the accidental foodie

For my mother, Pamela Whitaker (1935–1995)

the accidental foodie

neale whitaker

photography by petrina tinslay

MURDOCH BOOKS

contents

Preface 7

Introduction 8

Joan Campbell 22

Nigel Slater 32

Bill Granger 42

Tamasin Day-Lewis 52

Terence Conran 62

Jill Dupleix and Terry Durack 72

Cherry Ripe 86

Kevin Gould 96

David Thompson 106

Sybil Kapoor 116

Donna Hay 126

Peter Gordon 136

Claudia Roden 146

Maggie Beer 156

Antonio and Priscilla Carluccio 166

Stephanie Alexander 176

Neil Perry 186

Alastair Hendy 196

Darina Allen 206

Martin Boetz 216

Jamie Oliver 226

Index 237

His way was most certainly not the way of the solemn wine sipper or of the grave debater of recipes. Connoisseurship of this particular kind he left to others.

Elizabeth David (of the writer Norman Douglas)
as quoted in *An Omelette and a Glass of Wine* (Penguin, 1984)

preface

While I was researching and planning this book, I referred to the twenty or so people I have written about as my 'food heroes'. I never intended to call them that in the finished work for fear it might sound too fawning, but the phrase stuck. There is no better or more grown-up way of describing them, as that's exactly what they are. My food heroes. A diverse group of people that includes cooks, food writers, chefs, restaurateurs and stylists from both Britain and Australia. What they all share, and what links them in my mind, is an extraordinary passion for food and a lifelong commitment to bring better food within reach of all of us, through whatever means they have chosen. These people have inspired, influenced and taught me (and in just one or two cases, occasionally driven me crazy) on my own lucky journey through the world of food magazines. I am indebted to all of them.

Some people have queried my selection, wondering why I haven't included the likes of, say, the brilliant Nigella Lawson, Gordon Ramsay, Rick Stein or Fergus Henderson (who, if there was a straw poll amongst my food heroes — particularly the British ones — to nominate *their* food hero, would almost certainly win hands down). The answer is simple. My rationale was that everyone I wrote about had to have personally touched my own career at some point, albeit in some cases tangentially. That was my starting point and I hope the book is the more honest for it.

Along the way, there have been many other people that I would like to thank for their wisdom, encouragement and support. They include John Brown, Simon Brown, Ellen Brush, Jean Cazals, Michele Cranston, Elizabeth Crompton-Batt, Mia Daminato, Holly Davis, Matthew Drennan, Jane Druker, Sue Fairlie-Cuninghame, Russell Fish, Ken Gomes, Saska Graville, Felicity Green, Matt Handbury, Michael Hannan, Kendall Hill, Catey Hillier, Andrew Hirsch, Trudi Jenkins, Simon Johnson, Debbie Lewis, Lisa Linder, Valli Little, David Loftus, Jason Lowe, Geoff Lung, Andrea Lynch, Christine Manfield, Angela Mason, Karen McCartney, Barry and Karen McDonald, Michael McHugh, James Murphy, Dee Nolan, Mark Riordan, Deirdre Rooney, Daniella Shone, Janet Smith, Maurizio Terzini, Bill Tikos, Christopher Ward, Phil Webb, Martin Welch, Caroline West, Jon Whitaker, Stephen Whitaker and John Wilson.

Sarah Banbery was a genius with the sandwich maker all those years ago, and is still one of the finest cooks I know.

Cheryl Thomas showed me that a feast could be conjured from a potato, an onion and a measure of imagination.

Petrina Tinslay is a true food hero and no-one could have photographed this book better.

David Novak-Piper brought fun, love and delicious food back to my kitchen and continues to do so.

Neale Whitaker

introduction

Australia, February 1993: We sat for an hour in the Qantas lounge at Brisbane airport waiting to fly the last leg to Sydney. How crazy to fly so far and stop so close to the finishing post. I'd noticed that the runway controllers, the ones who bring the plane to rest waving those things that look like Ping-Pong bats, were wearing shorts. My very first memory of Australia. The hulking great Qantas jet lurching on to its stand just inches from their little legs and they were wearing shorts. But doesn't everyone in Australia? I suddenly remembered those Ladybird books from my childhood, the ones where two smiling kids with perfect side-partings and little matching suitcases wave to the friendly locals by the Taj Mahal one minute, Niagara Falls the next. Those Ladybird kids went to Australia and I'm sure everyone they met was wearing shorts. I must have been very jet-lagged. Later that night, and finally in Sydney, our taxi cruised the humid streets of Darlinghurst. I had an incredible sensation like goose bumps. I was in a strange city in a country I had never visited, knew nothing of, and frankly hadn't even wanted to come to, but I knew that I was undeniably, indisputably, home.

A career involving food was never on the cards. I announced to everyone at the age of seven that I was joining the merchant navy. I had absolutely no idea what the merchant navy was but I suspected it involved sailing to distant ports (maybe even Hong Kong, my childhood obsession) and possibly a smart uniform. It sounded unimaginably glamorous. I was very particular that it was to be the *merchant* navy, realizing even at that tender young age that I would be quite hopeless in combat. To this day I don't know who planted the idea in my young imagination, but the travel bug obviously bit early, if the palm trees I used to doodle all over my schoolbooks were anything to go by. Every now and then there would be a postcard on Grandma Bob's mantelpiece (for some unfathomable reason it was customary in our family for grandmothers to take on their husbands' names) from the enigmatic 'cousin Michael', usually posted from some remote exotic location. Grandma and great-aunt Ruby would always discuss unmarried cousin Michael in rather hushed tones. 'He's off with the Vogue girls again', I heard aunt Ruby say once. Even at seven I realized that the Vogue girls, unlike, say, the Rackham children or the Lillicrap kids, did not live around the corner. This was something much more highfalutin. Many years later, when I knew more about such things, I imagined cousin Michael as some stylish impresario who created wonderful fashion pages for *Vogue* magazine on distant shores. Perhaps he was a photographer, or a writer. Maybe he was a fashion designer or a fashion editor. A hairdresser? There were already a couple of those in the family — great-aunt Jill had a salon on Luton Road that reeked of perming lotion, and great-uncle Reg was a barber. Maybe unmarried cousin Michael just carried the suitcases for the Vogue girls. I never thought to ask.

But food? Not really. In the tradition of food writers, I feel obliged to say I learned to cook by my mother's side or at my grandmother's knee, but that would be absurd. My mother, whom I adored, taught me many important lessons in life, but culinary skills were only halfway up the list. And my maternal grandmother, Grandma Sid, whom I also loved dearly, appeared to survive on little more than Fray Bentos pies and frozen peas. As in so many English households of the 60s and early 70s, food was never a significant part of family life, which was all the more strange given that my own father and grandfather were fishmongers (R. C. Whitaker & Sons, fresh or 'wet' fish as they called it then, on one side of the shop, deep-fried with chips and a pickled egg on the other) and then greengrocers: R. C. Whitaker & Sons, fruiterers.

Meals just happened in our family, and their provenance was never questioned. My mother mightn't have seen it that way of course, but meals did just seem to appear at the appropriate time, and were never much commented on. Mum was a good, if plain, cook with a regular repertoire of solid English dishes. Curried beef with peanuts, sultanas, sliced banana and desiccated coconut; thick slices of pig's liver with fried onions, bacon and waxy boiled potatoes; sausage meat patties (a favourite of mine — deep satisfaction came with being served the patty that had stuck to the bottom of the pan in all its blackened, gooey glory); steak and kidney puddings and pies; minced beef shepherd's pie with buttery mashed potato and a good splash of worcestershire sauce. Mum's cakes were magnificent and there was always a jam sponge or some chocolate buns in the tin.

My extended family were food eccentrics. It was a tradition to eat bright yellow smoked haddock with tea and toast for breakfast — in deference to the family trade — and I assumed all families did the same. They didn't. Kippers yes, smoked haddock no. Great-aunt Violet apparently lived on air, despite her girth, while her spaniel gorged itself on fresh chicken. A younger aunt's speciality — usually as she lit her post-prandial cigarette — was a loud burp, much to the amusement of my brothers and me. And great-grandma Flo, who had clung tenaciously to her own name, kept her slippers on her feet with rubber bands and her peanut brittle in a Coronation tin, to be sucked (her teeth were usually absent without leave) while watching the wrestling on television. Flo's onion gravy could have sealed cracks in the wall but it was unspeakably delicious and I would keep my fingers tightly crossed that she would be compos mentis enough to make it for us. She seldom was.

I had unusual tastes for a young boy. Perhaps it was the shadow of France just a handful of kilometres across the English Channel (on a clear day you could see the French coast, and my grandfather used to joke that he could tell the time on the clock tower in Calais), but my idea of heaven was a 'continental' breakfast of warm croissants, salted butter and apricot jam. Perhaps more accurately, it was one of several ideas of culinary heaven I had as a child. Chinese takeaway from the Sea Palace restaurant next to the hospital was another, and I loved going to collect it in the car with my father. The Sea Palace reeked of stale prawn crackers, years and years of them. There was a huge Chinese lantern, yellowing tourist posters and a portable black and white television that the miserable woman behind the counter refused to take her eyes off, even while she handed us our silver-foil containers of number nine, number twenty-three and number thirty-seven. But in Margate, England, it was the closest I could get to Hong Kong.

Ground coffee bags — like tea bags — were all the rage in the early 70s and I thought they were the last word in chic, especially when the coffee was served with my mother's dinner-parties-only coloured sugar granules, and in her wobbly, hand-thrown coffee cups. Now I come to think of it, I thought my mother was the last word in chic too. Just occasionally we'd have 'astronaut food', dried meals (the brand was Vesta) that started life resembling the contents of the vacuum cleaner bag and transformed eerily into an approximation of a curry or chop suey with a cup of water, a few minutes on the hotplate and a large dose of imagination. I was sometimes allowed to cook the flat, dried noodles that were supposed to puff-up to golden curls in the frying pan, but invariably I'd have the pan too hot and the noodles would stick to the bottom like Band-aids. My poor, patient, mother must have despaired.

Memories of food, though not always memorable food, punctuate my childhood. Delicious poppy seed rolls from the kosher grocer for Saturday morning breakfast must have been delivered on Fridays. (We weren't Jewish, but the kosher grocer and his family were almost our neighbours; they lived in the house with the winking eye painted on the garage door which Mum, with some justification, thought vulgar.) Sometimes there would be a can of Bird's Eye Florida orange juice too, for a special treat. Corned beef and Branston pickle white-bread sandwiches stuffed with crushed-up potato crisps. My initials squeezed in tomato ketchup across a slice of my mother's eggy bread. And childhood ambrosia: fish fingers on toast. To this day I am unable to resist anything in breadcrumbs.

A visit to London, just two hours away, meant the velvet-rich sachertorte at the Swiss Centre in Leicester Square (you could choose from four underground restaurants — German, French, Italian and Swiss — all of which embodied the 'swinging' London of that era, like a subterranean, culinary Biba), while our summer holidays in Cornwall meant Cornish pasties fat with meat, potato and turnip and tall blue tins of the delicious local 'fairings': flat, chewy biscuits as wide as your hand, spicy with ginger and saffron-yellow. And because I was too old to be despatched early to bed (but too young for a social life of my own), I was always allowed a small taste of my mother's dinner-party food. 'Swiss steak' (what was this early-70s obsession with Switzerland?), a heady casserole of steak, onions and red wine that made me hungry to be an adult, and her fluorescent green apple mousse cake — a riot of food colouring — on a bed of crushed digestive biscuits and dusted with chocolate flakes. Did I mention that at ten, my age and my weight in stones were roughly the same?

If I'm tracking my foodie life, then the university years between 1980 and 1983 (where I harboured half-hearted dreams of being an actor) were a wasteland. My liver and mustard casserole achieved a certain notoriety but on the whole there wasn't much cooking. To be honest, we were all much more intent on spending quality time in the student union bar than worrying about food. We were all fairly dexterous with the can-opener and anything that could be boiled in its own little plastic bag. In the final months before graduation, my dear friend J and I fancied ourselves as Sebastian Flyte and Charles Ryder from *Brideshead Revisited* (which was showing on television at the time) and in the Charles role — to which I naturally inclined — I felt it was my duty to advise Sebastian that the drinking of his favourite Malibu and milk was very un-Evelyn Waugh. He instantly reverted to Bailey's, which we both agreed was sophisticated and respectable. After uni I wandered through India and South-east Asia for six months, also with J, where I became acquainted with flavours and cultures that have infused my adult life. It's funny to think that on my first encounter with coriander (my favourite herb) in India, I was violently repelled. I found it acrid and soapy and its sinister presence in what seemed like any and every dish sent my stomach into spasm.

That life-changing journey, made more than twenty years ago, recalls ambrosial coconut and banana porridge on Koh Samui, thick syrupy coffee with condensed milk (which I still love), toast with rancid butter at a roadside stop in Burma, soothing mugs of Milo that became our addiction in Malaysia's wet, miserable Cameron Highlands and the endless cry of the Indian chai sellers, plying their sweet, stale brew of boiled tea, milk, sugar and ginger. Our trip was almost entirely vegetarian, due mostly to the concerned entreaties of friends and relatives convinced that edible meat stopped at the English Channel. Perhaps they were right. An end-of-trip treat of chicken tikka in a grand old Delhi restaurant, against a backdrop of a sari-clad chanteuse performing 'Kung-fu Fighting' with a full orchestra, was followed by three hellish days of dysentery in a rat-infested hotel.

Back in London, I abandoned my plans to be an actor and resolved to work in fashion magazines. I ended up in public relations. A spell in the offices of PR guru Lynne Franks (who was to became the genesis of Jennifer Saunders's wonderful creation Eddie Monsoon in the cult comedy *Absolutely Fabulous*) introduced me to Buddhism, Boy George and macrobiotic food. My palate was growing. Later on, while working as the press officer for Browns, the swanky London fashion store, I ate foie gras in Paris at Angelina's on chic Rue de Rivoli, steak tartare at Le Caprice, tucked behind The Ritz in London, and escargots — what else? — at L'Escargot in Soho. I became as well acquainted with the pasta at San Lorenzo in Knightsbridge as Princess Diana. I was twenty-three years old with a dangerously high American Express bill, wore sunglasses in the front row at the Milan fashion shows (didn't everyone?) and thought happiness came in the shape of a Comme des Garçons suit. It was the 80s and I didn't give a shit. It seems that on my way to becoming the accidental foodie I had become an accidental prat.

The wonderful Felicity Green, the woman who taught me how to edit a magazine, is my mentor. When I met her in 1990 she was editing *The M&S Magazine* for the customers of Marks & Spencer, the retail giant that has always shared a unique place in the hearts and minds of the British. It was a quarterly magazine with a staggering circulation of almost two million. Green hired me as her deputy on little more than trust. I was 28 years old, had played around for far longer than I should have with the fashion and PR industries and had precious little to show on my publishing CV apart from a brief and unhappy stint at *Harpers & Queen* magazine. But I knew fashion and I'd learned how to handle difficult clients with diplomacy and kid gloves. That, and the fact that I'd already worked for Marks & Spencer as a fashion stylist, must have got me the job.

In 1990, Marks & Spencer was pushing the boundaries of food retail in Britain and *The M&S Magazine* of course had to reflect that. But food was the editor's territory, not mine. I busied myself with the fashion side of things while Green briefed food photographers and stylists, food writers and home economists (what on earth were they?) in the mysterious language of food and wine. For my part, I had no desire to wander the labyrinthine corridors of Marks & Spencer's offices in search of chicken Kievs and sticky toffee puddings. Food was not my comfort zone.

1993 was a year of change. In February, the magazine's art director and I flew to Australia as guests of Qantas and the Queensland Tourist Board to photograph fashion. We flew into Sydney with ten suitcases of clothes, met photographer Paul Westlake and our models and headed north to Queensland's beautiful Sunshine Coast where we shot in locations around Fraser Island, Noosa and its hinterland. Those ten days changed the angle of my career and my life. There was an immediate, intense bond with Australia. I remember sitting on Westlake's Potts Point balcony, nursing a restorative glass of wine (the jet-lag was hideous), with the Sydney skyline — the sails of the Opera House and the leviathan sweep of the Harbour Bridge — almost at my fingertips. I knew I was looking at my future home.

Back in London, I became editor of *The M&S Magazine* later that year. The magazine needed a rethink and Marks & Spencer was an impatient client. I missed Felicity Green's wise expertise. It was at this time that I first came across *Vogue Entertaining* (now called *Vogue Entertaining + Travel*)*,* an Australian cooking magazine that bore the familiar Vogue trademark I connected with catwalk fashion and luxury. On the pages of that magazine I found the brilliant clarity of light I'd experienced in Australia just a few months before, felt again the warmth and sunshine and tasted the fresh, simple flavours that I'd craved for weeks after my return to London. Through a unique combination of photography, recipes, layout and typography, *Vogue Entertaining* presented an Australian culture that, to a British eye, felt exotic, familiar and enticing all at once. Beautiful, natural food on simple white plates, food that looked and doubtless tasted of itself, with none of the elaborate artifice that I was familiar with. Ocean-fresh seafood and tropical fruits photographed in abundant sunshine that came free of charge. This was a different magazine to any I had ever seen. It felt liberated, relaxed, sexy and modern. *Vogue Entertaining* captured the basic joy of sharing good, simple, seasonal food, and presented it with a sophistication and visual flair that had traditionally been the domain of fashion and interior design magazines. There was nothing else quite like it — certainly not in Britain — and I was hooked. By a happy accident and without even realising it I became a foodie.

From a stylistic and attitudinal point of view, *Vogue Entertaining* influenced food publishing throughout the world. Whether it be the enduring legacy of simple, pared-back, modern presentation that allows the food to really star, or the more indulgent and passing vagaries of soft-focus food, vertiginous towers of food or food at alarming angles, most trends can be traced back to that magazine. Some of the world's most respected food photographers, such as Petrina Tinslay, Geoff Lung and Earl Carter, are Australians who cut their photographic teeth on *Vogue Entertaining*. Despite its relatively small circulation, few staff and a modest budget, *Vogue Entertaining* became a phenomenon, pioneering the way for a new generation of food magazines.

If I am an accidental foodie, then I am also an extremely lucky one. Few editors get even one opportunity in a career to create their ideal magazine. I have so far had two and I am grateful to passionate publishers like John Brown in London and Michael McHugh in Sydney for allowing ideas to take shape and then fly. Late in 1996, I landed at the door of maverick publisher Brown, who already published an eclectic portfolio of titles, from the satirical comic *Viz* to the languidly beautiful *Gardens Illustrated*. John Brown Publishing in those days was a young, fertile and liberal environment. Brown loved creative ideas and unusually for a publisher, even in 1996, he was willing to take a gamble. *Food Illustrated*, which eventually launched in March 1998, was born during a lunchtime walk along the Thames towpath with Brown. I was already editing a title for him, but he knew, from conversations we had already shared, that my ambition was to edit a food magazine in Britain that was truly different and equivalent to the great Australian titles that continued to inspire and influence. Brown wanted a companion title for the cult *Gardens Illustrated* he had created some years before. *Food Illustrated* seemed to meet both our needs.

In less than six months we had created a concept 'dummy' stuffed full of what we believed were new and different ideas. As editor-in-waiting and chief salesman (what Australians might call chief spruiker), I pounded the London streets with the dummy, cajoling some of the country's finest food minds into contributing to our launch issue. I was aware other magazines had occupied this territory before with limited success, but determination is a powerful drug and many of the amazing people I met at that time — writers, chefs, restaurateurs — are recorded on the pages of this book.

Food Illustrated was to be a new type of food magazine, one that went beyond recipes, menus and cooking techniques (although they were there in abundance) to capture and celebrate a passion for food ('it's all about passion ...' was the phrase that opened the introductory editor's letter), with stories from Britain and around the world. The first issue, which hit British newsstands in March 1998, contained a heady cocktail of features, from a review of London's first organic restaurant to food writer Sybil Kapoor's definition of modern British food to a photo-essay on cult New York deli Dean & DeLuca. There was a dinner party menu from interior designer *du jour* Kelly Hoppen, street food from Bolivia and a column in praise of chicken soup from the very non-Jewish Nigel Slater. The chef and writer Simon Hopkinson had written about two of his own food heroes, Francis Coulson and Brian Sack of Sharrow Bay Hotel in the English Lake District. Australia, of course, was well represented in that launch issue, with the first international magazine feature to be published on bills café in Sydney and its proprietor Bill Granger, and a 'foreign correspondent' column by the indomitable Joan Campbell, *Vogue Entertaining + Travel*'s food director.

When that first issue launched, our small team waited with a sense of defiant anxiety. We knew we had created the best magazine we could and if the public didn't appreciate it then the fault was surely all theirs. *The London Evening Standard* didn't like the magazine at all, describing it as food 'pornography'. That was a great phrase; we could work with that. Several other critics couldn't get their heads round our indulgent, full-page photographs of food, while others applauded them. I think someone described us as 'brave'. Fortunately, the verdict was overwhelmingly in favour of the new magazine and, while we couldn't exactly claim a victory at the newsstands (I think we might have given away more copies than we sold of that first issue), we seemed to have struck a chord with the industry. Now we just had to win over the British public — a notoriously difficult lot, weaned as they are on a diet of food slapstick and food nannying that can be traced back to the terrifyingly camp Fanny Craddock, who exemplified both. There were no jokes in *Food Illustrated*. Damn.

Food Illustrated published independently for twelve issues, gaining confidence and authority with each one. An overnight publishing sensation is rare, and we were naïve to expect that a magazine whose stock in trade was beautiful photography, intelligent food writing, frequently complex recipes and an opinionated stance on such issues as biodiversity, organics and genetic modification would achieve immediate commercial success. But what we hadn't foreseen was that we would come very swiftly to the attention of Britain's most prestigious and forward-thinking supermarket chain, who recognised that the magazine's values matched its own. Waitrose was *Food Illustrated*'s saviour and its involvement breathed life and support into the magazine. The first issue of the renamed *Waitrose Food Illustrated* hit the stands in April 1999, exactly one year after our launch, and is still published today, looking as handsome as it ever did. Some of those original contributors — writers such as Sybil Kapoor and Kevin Gould, and photographers like Jason Lowe and David Loftus — have remained fiercely loyal to the magazine, which might explain its enduring success.

One of the great things about life is that we never know exactly what's around the corner. It's all a game of chance. The moment I set foot in Australia in 1993 I fell in love with the vast country but would never have believed that in the space of a decade I would become an Australian citizen. It was a fantasy, but that's as far as it went. I was too old for a working visa and didn't have enough of those vital immigration points — I checked it out, several times. I had no ancestral claim to Australia (leastways that's what I thought) but it just felt right, it felt like home. Between 1993 and 1999 I must have made five or six trips, always to Sydney, and each time the itch got stronger. Sure, I loved London, my partner, my friends and family, my career, but there was a siren song calling.

On a practical level, I thought it would be good for my career. Having long admired the food and lifestyle books and magazines coming out of Australia and having witnessed their influence on publications around the world, I wanted to be at the centre of it. I craved what I perceived from afar as a relaxed, creative attitude, and publications infused with a lightness of touch dictated by climate and geography (naively, as it inevitably turned out — Australian publishing is as competitive, as ruthless and as driven by the all-important bottom line as its counterparts anywhere in the world, perhaps more so). I don't think I ever really believed that life in Australia would be like the pages of *Vogue Entertaining*, but after fifteen years in London, I was ready for a change and a new challenge. I'd rejected New York (too hard, like London on speed) and seriously considered San Francisco, even Los Angeles, but I kept coming back to Sydney. I needed my palm trees.

Early in 1999, I was contacted by Sydney publishers Murdoch Magazines, the publisher of Australian *marie claire* and the influential suite of Donna Hay's *marie claire* cookbooks. A new food magazine was on the drawing board and they thought I might be interested in editing it ... fate had intervened right on cue.

I was interested — very — but not immediately. There were a few loose ends in my life to tie up first. Six months later however, in October 1999, I was sitting in my own apartment in Sydney's Potts Point, looking at that magical city skyline. It was six and a half years, almost to the day, since I had sat before the same view on Paul Westlake's balcony and vowed to return. I have lived in Sydney ever since.

As a child I remembered Grandma Sid telling me of a distant relative from Australia. Sadly, I was never very interested at the time and anyone who could answer my questions now has long since left this world. But that memory kept playing on my mind and early in 2004 I asked a genealogist to trace my family ancestry. He discovered that my maternal great-great-grandfather, Robert Coulter (father of great-grandma Flo of the peanut brittle and onion gravy), was born in Sydney in 1843. Robert Coulter's own father had travelled to Australia from Britain sometime between 1812 and 1841. Robert obviously returned to Britain, as he married at the age of 40 in south-east London, but now I knew why Australia was in my blood. It explained the goose bumps.

About halfway through 2001, Australian publisher Michael McHugh at FPC Magazines suddenly got the green light from the ABC, the Australian Broadcasting Corporation, to launch a new food magazine (and importantly, a new type of food magazine) on its behalf. Negotiations had been drifting on for months, but once the deal had been rubber-stamped, everyone wanted the title on the newsstand the following week. Everyone, that is, except the editor-in-chief (me), who had a file of ideas and a bulging contact book but no staff. A quick calculation indicated that once staff had been hired we would have about four weeks to create the magazine. It reminded me of those crazy TV shows where a team of experts has to rebuild a house while the owner is out shopping.

The magazine was *ABC delicious.*, which hit the Australian newsstands in October 2001. When it launched in Sydney and Melbourne with speeches, sparklers, Champagne and a deafening blast of Kylie, we were unaware that we were christening one of the great success stories of Australian magazine publishing. The cover of the launch issue, photographed by Petrina Tinslay, was an irresistible stack of Bill Granger's buttermilk pancakes topped with chocolate fudge sauce and glistening thick cream. Set against a vibrant blue background (dispelling the old myth that blue and food should never mix on a magazine cover) with that distinctive silver logo — now one of the most visible magazine mastheads in Australia — *ABC delicious.* really did feel like a new type of food magazine. It was honest and down-to-earth, spoke to its readers like an old friend and was packed with chefs and food celebrities from TV Brits Jamie Oliver and Nigella Lawson to home-grown favourites like Granger, Elizabeth Chong, Ian Parmenter and our own food editor, the incomparable Valli Little. It was overflowing with recipes that were, quite simply, delicious, and it looked bloody good. For a magazine aimed at a mass audience it had the quality and polish of prestige titles. It was a simple formula but one that hadn't been seen before in Australia.

In the coming months and years, *ABC delicious.* and its near rival *Donna Hay magazine* (launched just a few weeks later) would vanquish the very magazines that had inspired them, once-dominant titles such as *Vogue Entertaining + Travel* and *Australian Gourmet Traveller*. The food publishing landscape in Australia is now changed, probably forever. It's an exciting new era and the gloves are off.

Maybe you shouldn't wish too hard. Isn't that what they say?

You might just get what you wish for. A year or so after the launch of *ABC delicious.* I found myself unexpectedly and temporarily in the editor's seat at *Vogue Entertaining + Travel*, as FPC Magazines acquired the licence to publish the *Vogue* magazines in Australia from Condé Nast. It was a time of huge change as two strong publishing cultures merged. From a personal point of view, it was a strange sensation to be suddenly at the helm of a magazine I had admired for so many years, but in an indelibly changed magazine landscape, it was also a great challenge. For more than a quarter of a century, *Vogue Entertaining + Travel* had been a remarkable and inspirational publication, the blueprint for food and lifestyle magazines around the world. I was just one of many editors throughout our industry whose career had been touched by it. But its real influence remains with the visionaries who launched and nurtured it in its early years. I have too much respect for them to claim any of its success as my own. I was an accidental editor.

'That's jellyfish you're eating,' said the matriarch of Australian cooking on our very first dinner date, and I swear I saw a twinkle in her eye. How could I have been foolish enough not to guess the sinister identity of the spicy rubber bands that were rapidly constricting my windpipe? But how could Joan Campbell have known that the sweaty-palmed Englishman opposite her had only one phobia in life — jellyfish? She couldn't know, could she? 'Lovely,' I squeezed out in a sort of falsetto death rattle, my innards rapidly heading north. Hopefully Joan would have read the tears in my eyes as those of sheer joy.

joan campbell

I once wrote in a British magazine that there was one woman who turned more heads than Elle Macpherson or Nicole Kidman when she walked into a Sydney restaurant and that was Joan Campbell, the legendary food director of *Vogue Entertaining + Travel* magazine. And I wasn't being flippant. From the few restaurants I visited with Joan on my early trips to Australia (the jellyfish incident occurred at Neil Perry's Wockpool, in Sydney's Potts Point), I could see that the octogenarian food editor was both feared and respected by the chefs and restaurateurs she had always championed. Never afraid to speak her mind, Joan's contempt for anything she considered pretentious or artificial was as withering as her praise could be lavish. At least one Sydney superchef had a dish dismissed by her as 'absolutely revolting' and dispatched back to the kitchen, quick-sticks.

Joan and her eldest daughter, the food editor and stylist Sue Fairlie-Cuninghame, have played a formidable role in establishing the might and influence of Australian food magazines. And it's hardly an exaggeration to say that Joan, who joined *Vogue Entertaining + Travel* shortly after its launch more than 25 years ago (when she was already well into her 60s) created those iconic magazine pages quite literally at her kitchen table. Not for her (or indeed for many Australian food editors) the luxury of photographic studios and a posse of stylists and

home economists. Instead, her recipes were created, tested and cooked by her in her own Sydney kitchen, carefully plated up (often under the watchful eye of the magazine's art director and later editor, Sharyn Storrier Lyneham) and then photographed — on a corner of Joan's dining table with only the magnificent Australian daylight for a backdrop. For many years, Joan and Sue worked closely together (Fairlie-Cuninghame was *Vogue Entertaining + Travel*'s executive food editor) and although tales of familial squabbling over the stoves are doubtless, like reports of Mark Twain's death, greatly exaggerated, Joan admits that working on a magazine with her own daughter 'had its moments'. A ringside seat at some of those cooking demos might have been priceless.

Her great friend, the writer and commentator Leo Schofield, describes Joan Campbell as 'an enormous force for good'. 'She had a vast amount of power in her role', he explains; 'she took a number of chefs under her wing and gave them confidence in what they were doing. She presented their food in a very glittering way.' But harnessing the talent of Australian chefs was only one side of the story. Campbell's own simple, honest, country cooking ('bush cooking' as she calls it; 'I'm a bush cook') was aimed directly at the Australian home cook. 'Joan's was a no-nonsense presentation which gave people confidence at a time when cooking was shrouded in mystery', says Schofield. 'She demystified cooking. I can recall going to the buffet and Joan would have a rack of lamb and a plate of ham on the table when everyone else was doing sloppy, messy stuff.'

Ever since jellyfish night, Joan and I have remained friends. True, I have never worked with her and so probably have been spared some of her infamous tongue-lashings, and I'm sure there have been a few times when, unbeknown to me, my judgement as an editor has come in for what might best be described as 'close Campbell scrutiny', but like most of us who have been connected to Joan, my respect and affection are very genuine. And she's one of the most wickedly funny people I know.

But heaven alone knows how she pulled her autobiographical cookbook *Bloody Delicious!* together in 1997. Her co-writer, Catherine Hanger, either had the patience of a saint or used hypnosis. Famously evasive about her age and the most reluctant of interviewees, Joan's favourite reply to most questions is 'I haven't got the faintest idea' and her observations on the Australian food stage and its cast are usually unrepeatable, let alone printable. Conversations in her Sydney apartment are punctuated by the frequent, uproarious shenanigans of her beloved poodle, Chandon, who takes, shall we say, a robust interest in male visitors, especially of the interviewing kind. But perseverance pays off. Joan Campbell has a vivid memory, especially when prompted by Sue.

'Food was the only thing that ever occurred to me to make a career of', she says, in a quiet moment with Chandon behind closed doors. 'And there have been times in my life too when I've had to cook to keep myself.' Interestingly, Joan speaks of the 'tyranny of distance', a phrase heard less often in modern Australia, but one relevant to her earlier years, when the continent's geographical isolation and vastness dictated cultural styles and identity.

Joan Campbell was born in Brisbane, Queensland, but spent much of her life in rural Queensland and New South Wales, always referred to as 'the bush'. 'In the bush there was the tyranny of distance as far as all but the most simple ingredients were concerned, but we always had gardeners, often recent migrants, who introduced me to exotics like capsicums and eggplants. We had asparagus beds, potato beds, olive trees, endless fruit trees and table grapes, wonderful tomatoes with real flavour, jerusalem artichokes and field mushrooms from the paddocks. We separated thick Jersey cream in our dairy and cut up sides of beef and hogget as we needed them. Country women are, and always have been, wonderful, generous cooks and great hosts. We all exchanged recipes and competed with each other.' Lucky the women who were on the receiving end of Joan's recipes, which still appear regularly in *Vogue Entertaining + Travel* and have so far

been collected in two books, the afore-mentioned *Bloody Delicious!* and *Five Minutes in the Kitchen*.

The Australian food scene that Joan Campbell presides over today is much changed from the one she inherited at *Vogue Entertaining + Travel* in the late 70s, and before that when she worked as a caterer, creating generous, memorable feasts for Leo Schofield and visiting luminaries such as Prince Charles and Pavarotti. There are the obvious changes (such as better produce and greater diversity) wrought simply by better communications, more knowledge and a more ethnically diverse population. But there are less tangible changes, too; an increased confidence, pride and sense of identity in modern Australian food. Joan has seen it all. She acknowledges 'how hard our chefs and food industry have worked at creating an Australian style and how successful so many of them now are and how respected around the world'.

Chandon re-enters the room and canine chaos returns. The questions need winding up. I ask Joan what she might say to the friends and colleagues who have described her as Australia's most influential food editor, hoping for a final hurrah of deep and personal reflection. 'Thank you very much', she says. 'What else do you expect me to say?'

joan campbell

duck salad

duck
1 Chinese barbecued duck or a
home-roasted duck
4 fresh kaffir lime leaves, finely
shredded
2 stems lemon grass, hearts only,
very finely sliced
30 g (1 oz/^{1}/$_2$ cup) fried garlic
flakes
6 spring onions (scallions), cut
in 2 cm (^{3}/$_4$ inch) lengths
1 tablespoon finely grated
fresh ginger

dressing
juice of 1–2 limes
2 teaspoons Thai fish sauce
2 teaspoons shaved palm sugar
2 tablespoons Thai sweet
chilli sauce

to serve
2 ripe mangoes, peeled, stoned,
flesh sliced lengthwise
leaves of 3 witlof (chicory/Belgian
endive), trimmed

To prepare the duck, remove all the flesh and skin from the duck, slicing in small irregular pieces, and transfer to a bowl. Add the lime leaf, lemon grass, fried garlic, spring onion and grated ginger.

To make the dressing, mix the lime juice, fish sauce, palm sugar and chilli sauce together in a small bowl.

To serve, drizzle the duck with the dressing and toss gently. Add the mango and witlof and turn through. Serve immediately.

Serves 6

whitebait with an asian flavour

batter
125 g (4¹/₂ oz/1 cup) self-raising flour
1 tablespoon peanut oil
1 tablespoon vinegar
250 ml (9 fl oz/1 cup) milk

500 g (1 lb 2 oz) fresh whitebait
3 tablespoons chopped coriander
(cilantro)
4 tablespoons finely sliced spring
onions (scallions)
1 tablespoon Thai fish sauce,
or to taste
very fine julienne of fresh ginger,
to taste
1–2 tablespoons finely sliced red
chilli, without seeds
peanut oil, for frying

garnish
coriander (cilantro) leaves
Thai fish sauce, for dipping

To make the batter, beat the flour, oil, vinegar and milk together until smooth. Rest for 1 hour.

For the whitebait, mix the whitebait, coriander, spring onion, fish sauce, ginger and chilli together.

Heat sufficient oil in a wide frying pan to shallow fry. Mix the whitebait through the batter and, without crowding, drop dessertspoonfuls into the hot oil. Drain on crumpled kitchen paper and serve as soon as possible, garnished with coriander and with fish sauce to dip.

Serves 4

joan campbell

prawn salad

salad
1 kg (2 lb 4 oz) cooked medium–large prawns, shelled and cleaned
560 g (1 lb 4 oz) can water chestnuts, drained and sliced
60 g (2¼ oz) pickled pink ginger, chopped if the pieces are large
200 g (7 oz/2 cups) shredded or julienne of green papaya
12 spring onions (scallions), finely sliced

dressing
200 ml (7 fl oz) coconut milk
125 ml (4 fl oz/½ cup) Thai sweet chilli sauce
1 tablespoon fish sauce

to serve
a large handful coriander (cilantro) leaves, picked over

To make the salad, place all the salad ingredients into a bowl, cover and refrigerate until serving time.

To make the dressing, put all the ingredients into a screw-top jar and shake until amalgamated.

To serve, add the coriander leaves to the salad, drizzle over dressing to taste, toss gently and serve at once.

Serves 6

joan campbell

summer strawberry soufflés

soufflés
butter, for greasing
icing (confectioners') sugar,
for dusting
400 g (14 oz) hulled strawberries,
crushed well
200 g (7 oz) caster (superfine) sugar
2 tablespoons Fraise de Bois liqueur
12 egg whites
pinch of salt
55 g (2 oz/$^1/_4$ cup) caster
(superfine) sugar, extra
icing (confectioner's) sugar,
for dusting

to serve
500 g (1 lb 2 oz) small strawberries,
hulled and puréed in a food
processor, with sugar to taste
whipped cream

To make the soufflés, generously butter ten 185 ml (6 fl oz/$^3/_4$ cup) soufflé moulds and dust with icing sugar. Cook the strawberries with the caster sugar over medium heat, stirring frequently, until the mixture is jammy, about 30 minutes. Stir in the liqueur, transfer the mixture to a bowl and set aside to cool.

Preheat the oven to 200° C (400° F/Gas 6).

Beat the egg whites with the salt and the extra 55 g (2 oz/$^1/_4$ cup) caster sugar until the mixture holds stiff peaks. Fold 2–3 large spoonfuls of the beaten egg white into the cooked strawberries to slacken the mixture and then fold in the remaining egg whites.

Spoon the soufflé mixture into the prepared moulds, levelling each with a spatula. Arrange the dishes on a baking sheet and then run the tip of your index finger around the edge of the mixture, down the side of the mould. This assists the soufflés to rise evenly.

Cook the soufflés on the centre shelf of the oven for exactly 12 minutes, remove from the oven and dust immediately with icing sugar.

To serve, one by one, split open the top of each soufflé, spoon in some puréed strawberries and whipped cream and serve at once.

Serves 10

Nigel Slater and I are roughly the same age, give or take a year or two. And we both grew up in the culinary wasteland that was England in the 1960s and 70s, he somewhere in the industrial middle and me on the south-east coast. *Toast*, the poignant autobiography Slater published in 2003 and which won him one of his many prestigious Glenfiddich Awards, vividly recalled my own childhood, though I doubt I could have conjured those years with such intimacy.

nigel slater

There are many things I've thanked Nigel Slater for over the years, but none more so than the opportunity to relive the taste of Walnut Whips, chocolate Nesquik, Angel Delight and the soft, comforting pap that was Mother's Pride bread. And to remember all those great British staples not with revulsion, but with deep affection and a strange sense of loss.

Despite *Toast*'s uncharacteristic self-revelation, Nigel Slater is a famously private man. The bespectacled and quietly spoken writer has penned a swag of very successful cookbooks with such titles as *Real Cooking*, *Real Fast Food* (into its 30th reprint) and *The 30-Minute Cook*. As the long-standing food editor of *The Observer*, he's probably done more than most world events to put that newspaper on British breakfast tables each Sunday. Of the food writers and chefs I met while pounding the London streets in mid-1997, clutching the proto-type pages of *Food Illustrated*, Slater was the one I wanted most to be impressed, the one I wanted most to like the idea. To my mind, his was the voice of New Food in Britain, honest food writing with impeccable left-wing credentials. He even had an Islington address. His name had to be on our first cover. I doubt he knows how nervous I was, sitting in his north London kitchen, and selling *Food Illustrated* for all the world like a market trader with a suitcase of fake Rolexes. But he was there in the first issue.

Fast forward seven years and Slater and I are once again sharing coffee and apple cake in his Highbury kitchen, except that this is a bigger kitchen in a much bigger house in a better neighbourhood. Slater is a successful man. The award-winning *Toast* is already in the hands of Hollywood scriptwriters, he's halfway through a promotional tour of the United States (which he's loathing on account of being separated from his beloved, but ailing, cat), and the next book is on the drawing board. Forgive the cliché, but Nigel Slater has come a very long way since his early days as a cook at a London deli called Justin de Blank. And on the journey he has taken a great many Brits with him, who perhaps see him as the quiet alternative to cooks with lisps or deep cleavages.

While Nigel Slater the man might shy away from the spotlight, his work has always been robust and confident. Before joining *The Observer*, he was food editor of British *marie claire* magazine, and the combination of simple, hearty recipes and bold, in-your-face imagery that he and photographer Kevin Summers created broke the mould of food presentation in Britain.

As Slater admits, his style was the antithesis of the soft-focus 'pictures on plates' that were still prevalent in food publishing in the late 1980s, a hangover from the nouvelle-cuisine era. 'I did this rustic, wobbly cooking which might be because I'm simply not a very good cook — most of my food's wobbly — but they [marie claire] loved it because it was new and it was real. We actually ate the food after we shot it.'

At a time when most food that went in front of the camera was rendered inedible by all the prodding, poking and painting, that would have been quite something. The images Slater produced, almost always photographed in the pan, defined the food of the period and whetted the appetite of an audience that was later satisfied by Slater's own cookbooks and the publishing phenomenon of London's River Café. It was in-your-face food photography with no attempt at artifice. Charred red capsicums drizzled with olive oil and balsamic vinegar, and torn basil leaves and glistening olives tossed casually through pasta, are images that have stuck with me.

If you've read Slater's columns over the years, in marie claire, then in The Observer, Food Illustrated, The Sainsbury's Magazine and his numerous books, you may share the image I have of a solitary man in love with his kitchen, his garden — and Britain. No matter how far he might stray into the flavours of India or Thailand, it's the Englishness that sticks. The puddings and pies, the cakes and roasts. When I ask him if he could ever imagine living anywhere other than England, or London, the response is surprising. 'Oh god, yes. I'm not terribly tied to Britain, not really. I would be very happy to live in Thailand and I'd happily live in India though I'd

have to live without cheese, which would be very difficult.' Surprising, too, is his personal belief that there is no real food culture in Britain, that 'it isn't part of our DNA. We're the magpies of the culinary world, we've always nicked other people's ideas, like the curry, the stir-fry, the pizza, but I'm not sure cooking is part of our soul in the way that it is for the Chinese, say, or the Italians.'

Despite his success, there's a hint of insecurity, which in a less humble, less likeable man might seem disingenuous. He describes his food as 'just something to eat, something nice for supper, no big message', adding that 'if you're a very serious cook you probably don't touch Nigel Slater'. The recipes he has written for a loyal audience in The Observer for twelve years are, in his words, like 'the big old pullover that has a few holes, but which you actually feel really comfy in'.

He is saddened by too much 'silly food' in food magazines. 'The sort of food where somebody has gone to the right place and taken the right photographs. Then they've come home and made the recipes fit. I love the idea of something in a beautiful bowl but I want to know that what's in that bowl has got integrity, that it's got a heart and a soul.' With Slater it's about honesty, and he welcomes the importance food lovers are increasingly placing on the provenance and pedigree of their food. 'If you're cooking for someone you love, you want to make sure that what you're giving them has a purity. Ten years ago I would go out and buy eggs and they were just eggs. Now I even know what the damn hen's name was, but I'm grateful for that.'

I like Nigel Slater enormously. I like his recipes, I like the engaging way he writes, and the way in which he can never quite make up his mind, like a schoolboy, about his Favourite Thing. In Slaterland, there might be nothing finer one week than a baked potato, while seven days later there will be nothing finer than a steak and kidney pie. Most of all I like the quiet, unassuming influence he has wrought on an industry that respects him. He is, perhaps, the Accidental Celebrity. 'I never, ever want to be the person where someone opens a magazine and says "Oh god, it's him again." ' No chance, Nigel, no chance.

'I could measure my life in quick pasta recipes. This recipe is not only a personal favourite but somehow sums up my whole ethos about cooking: simple, quick, bright tasting yet also somehow soothing and slightly indulgent.'

linguine with lemon and basil

200 g (7 oz) linguine
juice of 1 large lemon
80 ml (2¹/₂ fl oz/¹/₃ cup) olive oil
75 g (2¹/₂ oz/³/₄ cup) grated parmesan
a large handful of basil leaves

Put a huge pan of water on to boil. When it is bubbling furiously, salt it generously then add the linguine. Let it cook at an excited boil for about 8 minutes.

Put the lemon juice, olive oil and grated parmesan in a warm bowl (warmed under a running tap then dried) and beat briefly with a small whisk till thick and grainy. Tear up the basil and stir in with a grinding of black pepper.

Drain the pasta and quickly toss in the lemon and parmesan 'sauce'.

Serves 2

'My recipes tend to be simple and straightforward — the sort of cooking that anyone can do. Fish has always been my protein of choice and is invariably my first thought when I go food shopping. Tarragon is not most people's first choice with fish, yet other aniseed flavours work well, such as fennel, Pernod and chervil. It grows plentifully in my garden and it works beautifully here.'

haddock with crumbs and tarragon

two 200 g (7 oz) pieces haddock
120 g (4¼ oz) fresh(ish) white bread
8 anchovy fillets
a small bunch of tarragon
1 egg
a little plain (all-purpose) flour
pcanut oil and a thin slice of butter, for frying

Remove the skin from the fish. Tear the bread into chunks and reduce it to fine, soft crumbs in a food processor. Failing that, you could always grate the bread on the coarse blade of a grater. Rinse and pat dry the anchovies then chop them finely. Pull the leaves from the tarragon stalks then stir them into the breadcrumbs with the chopped anchovies and a grinding of salt and black pepper.

Crack the egg into a shallow bowl or deep plate and beat it lightly with a fork. Put a thick layer of flour in another plate, then put the seasoned breadcrumbs in a third. Dip the fish first into the flour, then into the egg and then, finally, the breadcrumbs. Pat the crumbs on both sides of the fish until each fillet is coated with a deep layer of herbed crumbs.

Warm the oil and butter in a shallow pan. May I suggest you make it a non-stick one? When the oil starts to sizzle, lower in the fish, leaving it to cook at an enthusiastic bubble until the underside is golden. Turn and cook the other side. It will need 3–4 minutes per side depending on the thickness of your fish. Test it by gently breaking off a piece.

Drain the fish on kitchen paper briefly before serving.

Serves 2

Above: haddock with crumbs and tarragon
Opposite: my very good chocolate brownie recipe

'Every cookery writer seems to have a brownie recipe and most of us quite naturally claim that ours is the best. This is one I have worked on over the years, getting just the right thin, crisp crust and the perfectly fudgy centre. No nuts, no flavourings, just a 24-carat brownie as dense as mud. Whatever else you add is up to you.
This recipe was originally developed for a piece I wrote about the Glastonbury rock concert.'

my very good chocolate brownie recipe

300 g (10^1/$_2$ oz/1^1/$_3$ cups)
raw (unrefined) caster (superfine)
sugar
250 g (9 oz/1 cup) butter
250 g (9 oz) chocolate (70% cocoa
solids)
3 large eggs plus 1 extra egg yolk
60 g (2^1/$_4$ oz/^{1}/$_2$ cup) plain
(all-purpose) flour
60 g (2^1/$_4$ oz/^{1}/$_2$ cup) finest-quality
cocoa powder
^{1}/$_2$ teaspoon baking powder
a pinch of salt

You will need a cake tin, about 23 cm (9 inches) square, preferably non-stick, or a small roasting tin.

Set the oven at 180° C (350° F/Gas 4). Line the bottom of the baking tin with baking paper. Put the sugar and butter into the bowl of a food mixer and beat for several minutes until white and fluffy. You can do it by hand if you want, but you need to keep going until the mixture is really soft and creamy.

Meanwhile, break the chocolate into pieces, set 50 g (1^3/$_4$ oz) of it aside and melt the rest in a bowl suspended over, but not touching, a pan of simmering water. As soon as the chocolate is completely melted, remove it from the heat. Chop the remaining 50 g into gravel-sized pieces.

Break the eggs into a small bowl and beat them lightly with a fork. Sift together the flour, cocoa, baking powder and salt. With the machine running slowly, introduce the beaten egg a little at a time, speeding up in between additions. Remove the bowl from the mixer to the work surface, then mix in the melted and the chopped chocolate with a large metal spoon. Lastly fold in the flour and cocoa, gently, firmly, without knocking any of the air out.

Scrape the mixture into the prepared cake tin, smooth the top and bake for 25–30 minutes. The top will have risen slightly and the cake will appear slightly softer in the middle than around the edges. Pierce the centre of the cake with a fork; it should come out sticky but not with raw mixture attached to it. If it does, then return the brownie to the oven for 3 more minutes. It is worth remembering that it will solidify a little on cooling, so if it appears a bit wet, don't worry.

Serves 12 (or 2 with the munchies)

'There were apple trees in the garden when I was a kid, and I have picked them for a living too; so it seemed only natural that old varieties of English apples should be the first thing I planted in my own garden. Four years old, they are now showing their first fruit. This cake is the first baking I did with those apples. A shallow cake, it is best served warm from the tin, but will keep for a day or two wrapped in foil.'

english apple cake

125 g (4^1/$_2$ oz/^{1}/$_2$ cup) butter
125 g (4^1/$_2$ oz) raw (unrefined) caster (superfine) sugar
3 'eating' apples
juice of half a lemon
^{1}/$_2$ teaspoon ground cinnamon
2 tablespoons raw (demerara) sugar
2 large eggs
125 g (4^1/$_2$ oz/1 cup) plain (all-purpose) flour
1 teaspoon baking powder
3 tablespoons fresh white breadcrumbs
a little extra raw (demerara) sugar (optional)

Set the oven at 180° C (350° F/Gas 4). Line the base of a 24 cm (9^1/$_2$ inch) square cake tin with a piece of baking (parchment) paper. I do this with one sheet of paper cut to the exact size of the base of the tin, but long enough to come right up the sides of the tin. That way you can just lift the paper to remove the cake.

Put the butter and caster sugar into the bowl of a food mixer and beat until light and fluffy. Whilst this is happening, cut the apples into small chunks, removing the cores as you go and dropping the fruit into a bowl with the lemon juice. Toss the apples with the cinnamon and raw sugar.

Break the eggs, beat them with a fork then add them to the butter and sugar. Sift the flour and baking powder together and fold them gently into the mixture. Scrape into the lined cake tin. Put the spiced apples on top of the cake mixture then scatter with the breadcrumbs and, if you wish, a little more of the raw sugar.

Bake for 55–60 minutes. You want the edges to be browning nicely and the centre to be firm. Leave to cool for 10 minutes or so before turning out. Eat warm.

Serves 8

nigel slater

friands $2⁰⁰
muffins $4⁸⁰

sparl'   ieral water ~ small $4⁴⁰ large $8⁵⁰
still   er ~ small $4⁴⁰ $4⁴⁰
coke $3⁵⁰
lemo $3⁵⁰

heine
as
cc
a   ⁵⁰
bi
ca

for wines by the glass
or full wine list
please see waiter
~corkage $6 per bottle

My friend Caroline took me to bills for an early-morning coffee in 1996. Every nerve in my English body resented being dragged out at such an unearthly hour (it was probably no earlier than 8.30, but I remember wondering why Australians so enjoyed these bizarre breakfast rituals) until I got to the cafe, where I promptly fell in love. Not with Caroline, although she's gorgeous, but with bills, as everyone does.

bill granger

Let me put this in perspective. bills (that defiant lower-case *b* is all part of the charm) is a café on a corner of a street in Sydney's shabby but fashionable inner-city suburb of Darlinghurst. It's small — not even 50 covers at full stretch — but its reputation is immense. People who have never even visited Australia have heard of bills. In a city as fickle as Sydney, where restaurants and cafés come and go like young soap stars, bills is an enduring beacon of good food, good coffee, good taste and sheer good looks. Since 1993, the sun has shone through those big old Darlinghurst windows onto polished wood floors, a scrubbed communal table, fresh flowers, a blackboard menu that remains unchanged (give or take the odd vagary of food fashion) and on to the café's owner himself, the upper-case Bill Granger.

When the first issue of *Food Illustrated* hit the stands in April 1998, it ran an eight-page feature on bills. Maybe it shouldn't have done. It might have been more politic to show British readers what was happening, café-wise, on their own shores rather than on the opposite side of the world, but I guess that as the magazine's editor I wanted to share my excitement about what was happening in the food scene in Australia and let some of that wonderful sunshine tumble on to the pages. I didn't consider that what Granger was doing in Sydney was irrelevant, and fortunately a generation of café owners agreed. The simple bills formula must be the most emulated, from Auckland to London to San Francisco to … Bury St Edmunds. On a recent visit to England, I stumbled upon a small café in the backstreets of that little market town in rural Suffolk, where the young owner proudly revealed Granger to be his hero. Granger remembers that original magazine article well. '*Food Illustrated* was the first big international coverage for bills. We had lots of people coming to the café with that magazine.'

Alongside his businesses (bills has a sister site in Sydney's Surry Hills), Granger's personal profile has grown remarkably. Now a familiar face on both sides of the globe through a successful TV series, a quartet of best-selling cookbooks and regular columns in such magazines as Australia's *ABC delicious.* and Britain's *BBC Good Food*, the man exudes charm. He's sunny, like his cafés. He is also a shrewd businessman who cleverly identified (ahead of his friend and compatriot Donna Hay) the untapped potential in simplicity.

'I'm not a chef, I'm not just a restaurateur, I'm not just a cookbook writer. What am I?' muses Granger in the cool office behind his original café. 'A bon vivant perhaps?' I'm not sure, but to my mind that phrase always conjures visions of wine-soaked, cigar-sucking excess. It would be hard to imagine anyone less like Sir Les Patterson than the almost cherubic Granger, who radiates the health and vitality most commonly associated with abstinence. But he certainly has the chutzpah of a bon vivant. A growing empire of cafés plus burgeoning media commitments and a demanding cookbook schedule demand a team of full-time administrative staff and a dedicated managing director. It's bills Inc.

'I've never just been interested in the food on the plate,' he explains. 'I'm interested in the interior of the restaurant, what the waiters are wearing, the whole package. What you *do* around food.'

Not surprisingly for a man whose passion is the entire experience, Granger cites Terence Conran as an important inspiration. 'He was the first visionary to tie it all up. I thought what he did was wonderful. I get the feeling that Conran likes eating in restaurants and so he simply creates restaurants that he likes. He's changed the way people eat and live, he's had so much influence.'

'My food is the food I like to eat, it's very much a personal thing,' he continues. 'I don't like processed food or complicated flavours. I'd much rather the clarity of real ingredients. I like things to be pared back.'

That food is the stuff that has kept Granger's customers coming back for more, and more. Everyone's a fan, everyone has a favourite bills breakfast dish, whether it's the renowned scrambled eggs (which prompted R. W. Apple in *The New York Times* to crown Granger as Sydney's 'egg master'), the equally famed pillows of ricotta hotcake served with fresh banana and rich honeycomb butter, the corn fritters with roasted tomato or the delicate lunchtime linguine with fresh seafood. 'People got upset when we tried to change the menu!' he jokes, 'but the great thing about breakfast is that it's not a fashion meal, it doesn't change. We all still want pancakes and scrambled eggs.'

Many an Australian celebrity has 'fessed up to a bills craving while overseas. Donna Hay, vying with Granger as the country's unofficial lifestyle ambassador, has admitted bills is the first place she heads for when she returns home to Sydney. And when food writers Jill Dupleix and Terry Durack moved to London, finding a local equivalent of bills was a priority. They didn't.

Granger is often described as a quintessential Sydneysider, and (despite the fact that he's originally from Melbourne) he does seem to embody the energy and optimism of his adopted city. His three young daughters — Edie, Ines and Bunny — were all born in Sydney and despite the pull of Europe, where he spends increasingly more time, Granger's heart is in the harbourside city. 'London would be fun but I love the quality of life here, I love being able to swim every morning or walk along the beach. It's grounding and important to me. When I moved from Melbourne I fell in love with the casualness of Sydney. It's a seductive city where the skies are always blue. Sydney really made me embrace my Australian identity. I'm passionate about Australia.'

There are many appealing things about Bill Granger, but most attractive is his optimism. So many of his sentences start with 'The great thing about ...'. This man loves his life and what he's doing with it. Is he ambitious? Driven? You will rarely hear a criticism of Granger, but on that rare occasion it might just be about control, often the Achilles heel of the creative.

'In the early days I just wanted to open a little café but yes, I was quite driven. I used to hate working for other people because I couldn't control it. I always had a strong vision of the way things should be, from the chairs to the food to the way it was served – everything. I love things to be beautiful. Food *is* beautiful.'

I ask him what he hopes the next decade will bring. 'Hopefully I will still be making good food accessible to everyone. I think that once you've tasted good health and eaten fresh, clean food, it's really hard to ever go back.' He looks thoughtful for a moment. 'If I could have a farm in the middle of the city that would make me very happy.'

scrambled eggs

2 eggs
80 ml (2$^{1}/_{2}$ fl oz/$^{1}/_{3}$ cup)
pouring cream
a pinch of salt
10 g ($^{1}/_{4}$ oz) butter

Place the eggs, cream and salt in a bowl and whisk together.

Melt the butter in a non-stick frying pan over high heat, taking care not to burn it. Pour in the egg mixture and cook for 20 seconds, or until gently set around the edge. Stir the eggs with a wooden spoon, gently bringing the egg mixture on the outside of the pan to the centre. The idea is to fold the eggs rather than to scramble them. Leave to cook for 20 seconds longer and repeat the folding process. When the eggs are just set (remembering that they will continue cooking as they rest), turn out onto a plate and serve with hot toast.

Serves 1

If you are making more than two serves of scrambled eggs, make sure you cook separate batches so as not to crowd the frying pan.

bill granger

lobster sandwich

lime mayonnaise
125 g (4$^{1}/_{2}$ oz/$^{1}/_{2}$ cup) mayonnaise
2 tablespoons fresh chives
2 tablespoons lime juice
sea salt
freshly ground black pepper

1 loaf white sandwich bread
800 g (1 lb 12 oz) lobster, cooked
and sliced (prawns are also
delicious)
1 Lebanese (short) cucumber,
peeled and finely sliced
1 large handful of coriander
(cilantro) leaves, loosely packed

To make the lime mayonnaise, mix the mayonnaise with the remaining ingredients and season well with salt and pepper. Spread a layer over one side of half of the slices of bread and then top with alternating pieces of lobster, cucumber and coriander. Put the remaining bread slices on top, and serve.

Serves 4

coconut bread

2 eggs
300 ml (10¹/₂ fl oz) milk
1 teaspoon vanilla essence
310 g (11 oz/2¹/₂ cups) plain
(all-purpose) flour
2 teaspoons baking powder
2 teaspoons ground cinnamon
230 g (8 oz/1 cup) caster (superfine)
sugar
150 g (5 oz/2¹/₄ cups) shredded
coconut
75 g (2¹/₂ oz) unsalted butter, melted

to serve
butter
icing (confectioners') sugar

Preheat oven to 180° C (350° F/Gas 4). Lightly whisk eggs, milk and vanilla together.

Sift the flour, baking powder and cinnamon into a bowl, add the sugar and coconut and stir to combine. Make a well in the centre and gradually stir in the egg mixture until just combined. Add the melted butter and stir until the mixture is just smooth, being careful not to over-mix.

Pour into a greased and floured 21 x 10 cm (8¹/₄ x 4 inch) loaf tin and bake in the preheated oven for 1 hour, or until bread is cooked when tested with a skewer.

Leave in the tin to cool for 5 minutes, then remove to cool further on a wire rack. Serve in thick slices, toasted, buttered and dusted with icing sugar.

Makes 8–10 thick slices

free-range chicken schnitzel with tomato and preserved lemon salad

4 free-range skinless, boneless
chicken breasts
160 g (5³/₄ oz/2 cups) fresh
breadcrumbs
10 g (¹/₃ oz/¹/₄ cup) chopped parsley
20 g (²/₃ oz/¹/₂ cup) chopped chervil
10 g (¹/₃ oz/¹/₄ cup) chopped
oregano leaves
1 teaspoon sea salt
freshly ground black pepper
2 eggs
125 ml (4 fl oz/¹/₂ cup) milk
250 g (9 oz/2 cups) plain
(all-purpose) flour
1 tablespoon butter
80 ml (2¹/₂ fl oz/¹/₃ cup) olive oil

tomato and preserved lemon salad
4 apollo tomatoes or salad
tomatoes, cut into wedges
4 spring onion (scallion) bulbs,
finely sliced into rings
20 g (²/₃ oz/¹/₂ cup) parsley,
thinly sliced
¹/₂ bunch watercress, picked over
2 tablespoons olive oil
1 tablespoon lemon juice
1 tablespoon preserved lemon, diced
50 ml (1¹/₂ fl oz) white wine vinegar

Place chicken breasts on a chopping board and lightly flatten out with a meat mallet. Put the breadcrumbs, herbs, salt and pepper in a bowl and mix well. Put the eggs and milk in another bowl and beat lightly together. Put the flour into a separate bowl.

Dip chicken first in the flour, then the egg mix and finally in the breadcrumb mixture. Continue until all chicken is coated.

Heat the butter and olive oil in a large non-stick frying pan over medium heat. Place enough chicken in the pan to cover the base — be careful not to overcrowd. Cook for 3–4 minutes, or until golden brown on one side. Turn over and cook a further 3–4 minutes. Remove from pan and keep warm until all the chicken is cooked.

For the tomato and preserved lemon salad, place all ingredients in a bowl, season with black pepper to taste and gently toss.

To serve, divide the salad among four plates. Place the warm chicken on a chopping board and cut into halves. Arrange chicken on plates with the salad and serve.

Serves 4

bill granger

Tamasin Day-Lewis and I disagree about how we met. I prefer my version. Early in 1998, I read an extract from her beautiful book *West of Ireland Summers* in a British Sunday newspaper and was struck by the easy, lyrical way in which she combined food, place and memory. There was a quality in Tamasin's writing that urged me to track her down, convinced that hers was exactly the sort of voice we needed in *Food Illustrated*. The more prosaic Day-Lewis version of events is that she tracked me down, after a girlfriend saw an ad for the magazine in the Sunday paper, and suggested there might be some work going.

tamasin day-lewis

Whatever, meet each other we did, and I discovered that this Anglo-Irish woman with her wild hair and darkly patrician looks, English public school diction and an addiction to Manolo Blahnik shoes was as captivating in life as on the page. Tamasin Day-Lewis's quietly incisive profiles of such food luminaries as Nigella Lawson, Egon Ronay, restaurateur Alastair Little, American food critic Jeffrey Steingarten and her great friend, the Irish chef Richard Corrigan, became a regular component of the magazine.

Later on, I found we shared an unusual bond. Tamasin's great mentor is the late English cook and restaurateur George Perry-Smith, whose Bath restaurant, The Hole in the Wall, is revered in English food lore. She met Perry-Smith several times and admits she 'owes nearly everything' to him. In his later years, Perry-Smith ran a restaurant called The Riverside at Helford, in a remote corner of Cornwall in England's far south-west. My own childhood holidays were spent in that region, and on more than one occasion (and probably around the same time as a young Tamasin Day-Lewis paid her first visit) I can remember my parents taking us to The Riverside for an end-of-holiday treat. Unlike Day-Lewis, my 13-year-old self was blissfully unaware of who was cooking my lunch and I can scarcely remember what I ate yesterday, let alone in 1975, but she assures me it would have been nothing less than Perry-Smith's customary 'wonderful food without rigmarole'. Maybe even his signature dish of salmon en croute with ginger and currants.

More recently, on an autumn evening in the kitchen of her 16th-century farmhouse in Somerset's gentle Quantock Hills, Day-Lewis is preparing us a dinner of grouse (she had phoned me in London in a panic that morning, strangely convinced that Australia had turned me vegetarian) and organic root vegetables pulled from her garden. Her mood is by turns combatant, then relaxed. She gets angry very quickly about a lot of things, mostly food related, but she knows when she's ranting and the wonderful throaty laugh that my mother would have described as 'filthy' is the ritual sign-off. She detests the interference of what she calls the 'food police', legislative bodies that threaten the livelihood of artisanal food producers ('nobody has ever died from eating an unpasteurized cheese') and the British supermarkets come in for a left hook. 'They're terrible, completely terrible, and what they've done is destroyed people's understanding of what food should taste like.'

We are sharing a bottle of the best (in fact, the only) Champagne I could find in the village general store. '*Slainthe*!' (Gaelic for 'cheers') she laughs, taking a momentary break from the Aga. Chancing my luck, I ask if she considers herself a food activist as Darina Allen in Ireland and Stephanie Alexander in Australia do. She almost chokes on her Möet. 'The moment I hear something like that I want to rebel!' Despite being a great fan of both Allen and Alexander, she finds labels 'ludicrous'. 'If I called myself a food activist I'd just think I'd completely lost the plot, that I was taking myself far too seriously.' If not an activist, Day-Lewis will at least admit to being a 'food fascist', which to my ear sounds far more sinister.

She decided at university that she was 'never going to eat bad food again' and her insistence on quality and integrity borders on the fanatical. By her own admission she's 'obsessive' about everything and thinks nothing of driving twenty, thirty, forty miles for the perfect cheese or loaf of bread.

Yes, of course her kids (she has three — Harry, Miranda and Charissa) had fish fingers and baked beans when they were young but the beans were soaked at home and the tomato sauce was fresh and organic. 'When they had friends round, I'd make an incredible home-made pizza with my own organic dough and they'd say "Please, Mrs Organic, can't you stop? Why can't you pull something from the deep-freeze like normal mothers do?".'

There was never an intention to make a career from food, despite a childhood infused by it. She recalls early trips to her beloved County Mayo. 'Turnips, cabbage, onion, carrot, potato, Irish stew, more Irish stew. Dan [her brother, the actor Daniel Day-Lewis] and I would catch mackerel and sell them on the quay for a penny each.' After graduating from Cambridge University, Day-Lewis, the daughter of the late English poet laureate Cecil Day-Lewis, worked first in television and then became a film maker. 'I was always passionate about cooking but I never thought I would know enough or want to do it enough to make a living from it. I'm still learning how to cook now.' Her career as a food writer is relatively new, growing from the success of her books (she has published five since 1997) and her columns in the weekend edition of Britain's *Daily Telegraph*.

But in conversation, she often gives the impression that she struggles with her role as a food writer. She can sound strangely apologetic. 'Food writing isn't really a serious profession. People are always saying to me "When are you going to write your novel?", as if what I'm doing is a little, *de trop*.' One wonders whether the family name weighs a little too heavily on her shoulders. Her kitchen bookshelves groan with the works of the writers she admires, such as Claudia Roden, Marcella Hazan, Simon Hopkinson, Jane Grigson, Elizabeth David and M. F. K. Fisher. These are the people whose food has the integrity and simplicity she demands of her own work. When I point out that the last three are long dead and that she might consider taking on one of their mantles herself, my suggestion is quickly rebuffed. But despite her protestations, Day-Lewis's writing for me holds the heady mix of memory, place and tradition that infused Elizabeth David's. Ireland is Day-Lewis's Mediterranean and her evocations of the brooding County Mayo landscape are spellbinding.

'I'm inspired by traditionalists who haven't actually lost sight of what good food is all about,' she explains, when we talk about her inspiration. The afore-mentioned Richard Corrigan and Marcella Hazan fall into this category. A handful of contemporary chefs who are caught up with 'froths and lathers and other gruesome things' are dealt the same mischievous short shrift as the food police. 'I think it's all bullshit.' Day-Lewis's own food philosophy (probably not a term she would use) is to 'find the best ingredients and do as little to them as possible, just make them taste more of themselves'.

'I believe that food is one of the most important things in life. There is certainly no gesture you can show anyone of greater love than cooking them a good dinner.' Over the sublime grouse, our conversation takes a gently wine-soaked meander through sonnets (she loves to write them), world meat consumption ('more dangerous than nuclear power') and Jamie Oliver ('he's made a whole generation of people like my son Harry think it's cool to cook'). Then we get to cheese. The Day-Lewis eyes flash. 'We are so ignorant about it ['we' being the majority of people in Britain, maybe the world, but not us], we don't even know how to put a cheeseboard together. We don't know whether you should have a mature sheep's next to a fresh goat's. *What's wrong with us?'*

It's a rant, and a good one.

'The all-time comforter of dishes, as good with guinea fowl as it is with a succulent, organic, free-range chicken. The chicken is poached gently in stock, the sauce made with white wine, stock, thick cream, gruyère and French mustard, but the real guts of the dish comes from a confetti of tarragon, so much you think it's sheer madness but it isn't.'

chicken savoyarde

for cooking the chicken
One 2 kg (4 lb 8 oz) organic chicken
2 onions, peeled, and one of them stuck with 2 cloves
2 carrots, peeled, halved lengthways
3 sticks of celery, chopped in half
2 leeks, trimmed and well washed
2 bay leaves
2 sprigs thyme
salt

for the sauce and to finish
50 g (1³/₄ oz) butter
50 g (1³/₄ oz) plain (all-purpose) flour
400 ml (14 fl oz) poaching stock
300 ml (10¹/₂ fl oz) dry white wine
250 ml (9 fl oz/1 cup) thick (double/heavy) cream
100 g (3¹/₂ oz/³/₄ cup) grated gruyère cheese
1 tablespoon dijon mustard
50 g (1³/₄ oz) tarragon leaves, chopped
salt and pepper
55 g (2 oz/²/₃ cup) fresh breadcrumbs
25 g (1 oz/¹/₄ cup) grated parmesan cheese

Put the chicken in a large pot with the vegetables, herbs and salt. Poach very gently for about 1¹/₂ hours, skimming off any scum that comes to the surface. Once cooked, lift out the bird and allow to cool. Strain the stock through a fine sieve and discard all solids. Leave to settle and lift off any surface fat using several sheets of absorbent kitchen paper.

Remove all meat from the chicken carcass (discarding the skin and also removing all sinews from the drumsticks) and cut into large, bite-sized pieces.

To make the sauce, melt the butter in a pan, add the flour and cook for 3 minutes without browning. Gradually add the hot poaching stock, white wine and cream and stir until thickened. Stir in the gruyère cheese, mustard and tarragon, correct the seasoning and simmer all together for about 20 minutes.

Preheat the oven to 230° C (450°F/Gas 8). Put the chicken in a buttered gratin dish, pour over the sauce and sprinkle with the breadcrumbs and parmesan cheese. Bake in the pre-heated oven for 20–25 minutes until the dish is golden brown and bubbling well around the edges. Eat with buttered new potatoes and a crisp green salad.

Serves 6

'I've written a book about tarts, but if I were to choose one tart, the be-all and end-all of tarts, this would be it. It has that Provençal tone of olive oil scented with fresh herbs, basil, parsley, rosemary and thyme. It has a hit of dijon mustard and a goo of gruyère to surprise you with. And the top deck is a painting in itself; rows of ripe tomato interspersed with creamy-salt goat's camembert painted with herby oil. A broad bean and asparagus salad would dress it up, a simple green one would dress it down.'

tomato, goat's camembert and herb tart

herbed brushing oil
125 ml (4 fl oz/¹/₂ cup) extra virgin olive oil
2 teaspoons each of finely chopped rosemary, thyme, basil, fennel and flat-leaf (Italian) parsley
1 clove garlic, crushed
salt and black pepper
1 bay leaf

shortcrust pastry
270 g (9¹/₂ oz/2¹/₄ cups) organic plain (all-purpose) flour
80 g (2³/₄ oz) unsalted butter
2 tablespoons extra virgin olive oil, or as needed

filling
1 tablespoon dijon mustard
100 g (3 ¹/₂ oz/³/₄ cup) gruyère cheese, grated
1 dozen or so organic tomatoes, sliced
four 125 g (4¹/₂ oz) camembert-style goat's cheeses, such as Soignon or Millerwood, sliced

Combine all the ingredients for the brushing oil in a jar or bowl and leave overnight if possible, or at least for a couple of hours.

Make the shortcrust pastry using your best olive oil instead of water — you might need a bit more than 2 tablespoons. Chill, then roll out and line a 30 cm (12 inch) tart tin.

Preheat the oven to 190° C (375° F/Gas 5) and put a baking tray in the oven.

Spread the mustard over the pastry base, then scatter over the gruyère. Cover with alternate overlapping slices of tomato and goat's cheese in concentric circles, then brush two-thirds of the herby oil over the surface. Bake the tart on the preheated baking tray for about 35 minutes; it will be heaving, brown and bubbling. Remove from the oven, brush with the remaining oil and leave to cool for at least 10 minutes before turning out and serving.

Serves 6 for supper, 8 for lunch

Opposite: tomato, goat's camembert and herb tart
Above: sicilian capsicums

'The simplest of starters to remind you of the heat and summer sun (that you never get in England!). Heaving with garlic, anchovies, parsley and your best peppery olive oil, it can be left in your fridge for a week and produced when the hordes descend unexpectedly.'

sicilian capsicums

4 red capsicums (peppers)
1 onion, finely sliced
2 cloves garlic, chopped
3 tablespoons best extra virgin olive oil
sea salt
half an organic vegetable stock (bouillon) cube
2 tablespoons best balsamic vinegar (aged, velvety, black and mellow)
small bunch fresh oregano
18 best glossy black olives, halved and pitted
4 anchovy fillets in olive oil
1$^{1}/_{2}$ tablespoons salted capers, rinsed under a cold tap
black pepper

Grill or char your capsicums until they are uniformly blackened and softened. Leave them to cool, then the skins should peel away easily. Cut the prepared capsicums into long strips.

Cook the onion, garlic and olive oil gently in a covered pan, with a bit of salt and a couple of tablespoons of water. You want the onion to be softened to a purée. Remove the lid and continue cooking until the onion is golden, which will take about 40 minutes. Add the strips of capsicum, the crumbled stock cube and the balsamic vinegar. Cook, uncovered, for a further 30 minutes, stirring occasionally. Add an extra tablespoon or two of water if the mixture seems to be drying out.

Add all the other ingredients, and carry on cooking for 20 minutes at a very low temperature; anything more and the anchovies will turn bitter.

Serve the capsicums warm or at room temperature with good crusty bread, or with game or cold roast meat.

Serves 4

'My cooking life has always been about a kitchen that my best cooking friends can cook in with me. We plan our weekends like culinary military campaigns. Dishes emerge as we discuss how and what we are going to do by a sort of osmosis. This sensational ice cream started because we couldn't be bothered to make a torta di Santiago. *The almonds and the quince paste remained, the rest was dreamt up on the spot.'*

quince and pralinéed almond ice cream

225 g (8 oz) quince paste (membrillo)
2 tablespoons lemon juice
1 tablespoon water
1 tablespoon Oloroso or other sherry
290 ml (10 fl oz) thick (double/heavy) cream, Jersey if possible
140 g (5 oz) blanched whole almonds
55–85 g (2–3 oz) raw (unrefined) caster (superfine) sugar

Melt the quince paste gently in a pan with the lemon juice, water and sherry.

Whisk the cream until it holds softly but isn't stiff.

In a non-stick frying pan over a gentle heat, scatter the almonds in a single layer and pour the sugar over them. Stir as the sugar melts and the brittle turns the colour of butterscotch, but not dark brown. Remove from the heat instantly and pour onto a greased baking tray. Leave to solidify, then bash into small chunks and little shards.

Fold the cream into the membrillo mixture, then fold about one-third of the brittle into it and freeze. Transfer to the fridge for 30 minutes before serving and offer a bowl of the remaining brittle to scatter sparingly over the top.

Serves 4–6

tamasin day-lewis

terence conran

I have two sheets of paper dated March 9, 1998 and headed simply '*Food Illustrated*: Comments'. It is a page-by-page critique of the first issue and the comments, addressed to the magazine's publisher, John Brown, run the gamut from 'quite dull' (page 19, a restaurant review written by someone called Neale Whitaker) to 'dull' and 'okay'. The contents page got a 'quite nice and clear' while — thank the lord — food writer Simon Hopkinson's paean to the late Francis Coulson's sticky toffee pudding got a 'good, charming and different'. The feature on Sydney's Bill Granger got 'excellent, very tasty', which reminds me that this particular critic has always admired the Australian way of doing things. Overall, the critic claimed that he 'liked the whole feel of the new magazine' but thought that the content was 'too thin'. 'It need not be as wordy as *Vanity Fair* or *The New Yorker* but I really do need more information.' In the next issue, he got it. When Sir Terence Conran critiques your magazine, you listen.

There is something about Terence Conran that makes you straighten your tie, shine your shoes and speak properly. You sense that he would never dream of doing anything less for you. And perhaps it's a mark of good old-fashioned respect that, heading out of London to his English country estate on one of those dreary half-light autumn days, I felt a nervous compulsion to over-rehearse my questions and practise my body language. God knows what they thought of me on the 9.05 to Kintbury. But in conversation with a lifestyle guru more than thirty years one's senior, does one relax into one's chair, suggesting equal terms, or does one cling to the edge of one's seat like an eager cub reporter? And heaven forbid that he remember me as the writer of dull restaurant reviews.

I don't believe Terence Conran actually coined the phrase 'lifestyle', but he invented the concept, familiarized us all with it and embodies it. Through his Habitat retail empire in Britain, his international network of hotels, restaurants and bars and the iconic Conran Shops, he has championed the appreciation of quiet good design and integrity, the global influence of which, from retail and publishing to restaurants and interior design, has been immeasurable. His detractors might occasionally condemn 'Conranization' as sophisticated homogeneity, especially of the London restaurant scene, but I personally believe Conran raised the British bar and helped redefine Britain — and London in particular — as a proud and innovative food capital.

Terence Conran (he was knighted in 1983 but prefers to be called Terence) is 74 years old. That's a significant fact when you pause to consider the company he might have kept in his lifetime — the writers and artists, the socialites and designers — but irrelevant so far as his current work is concerned. A conversation with this man, who has famously said he will never retire, feels stimulating, contemporary and connected. He also has a quite remarkable memory.

I had always thought that Conran's involvement in restaurants was a logical extension of the Habitat home furnishings business he founded in 1964. Not so.

It turns out his relationship with food started with a humble career as a *plongeur* — a washer-upper — in a Paris restaurant in the early 1950s, where he discovered (and he says this with a twinkle in his eye) that 'chefs were incredibly unpleasant rogues and thieves'.

That fact didn't deter him from opening a café called The Soup Kitchen on his return to London, which served four different types of soup, French bread ('unknown in London at that time') and a 'very good apple flan made by a Mrs Truman in Bethnal Green.' But The Soup Kitchen's secret ingredient was London's second espresso coffee machine (a second-hand Gaggia brought back from Turin) that must have seemed exotic beyond belief in the post-war London of fifty years ago. (London's first machine was apparently at a Knightsbridge café called Mocambo, and I suspect this is the only time in Conran's career that he has been second off the mark.)

Conran has a wonderful and often mischievous turn of phrase delivered with the careful diction of a bygone Britain (at one stage in our conversation he mentions living 'orf the land'). When I ask him what first drew him to food, he pauses for just a moment before replying, 'My mother. She placed me on her tit and said suck!'. Guffaws of laughter. He claims that through those impecunious months in Paris as a very young man, with his arms in the sink, 'the cockroach got into the bloodstream and it just made me fascinated about restaurants. The theatre of restaurants is very important

indeed, the excitement you get from seeing a restaurant full of people having a good time, it's like an actor standing on a stage looking at the audience.' Thinking of some of the 'theatres' that Conran has created over the years, such as Quaglino's and Mezzo, reputedly Europe's largest restaurant when it opened in 1995, you realise just how profound the effect of those Paris days must have been. That said, he has also enjoyed the way in which his various careers as restaurateur, designer, furniture manufacturer and retailer have all dovetailed into each other.

Like so many of the people I spoke to while writing this book, on both sides of the world, Conran cites Elizabeth David as an important inspiration (she was the only food writer whose books could keep him up in bed reading 'with a pretty girl beside me', which I guess is a compliment to David) along with Michel Guerard and Jane Grigson. He admits that he is 'of the very rigid and rather boring camp' whose lifelong influence has been the 'delicious food, very simply prepared' that he found in the cafés of France immediately after the war. He can still conjure (and so can I, hearing his description) the best meal of his life at a restaurant recommended by Elizabeth David, Madame Barratero's Hotel du Midi at Lamastre in France. 'It was chicken in a pig's bladder with black truffle under the breast, and when it came to the table they cut it open and the steam nearly knocked you over. I just remember this chicken with some little new potatoes and a big bowl of *haricots fines*. We had half the chicken for supper and the other half cold for lunch the next day.' I suspect the dish Conran so vividly recalls is Madame's *poularde en vessie* that David describes in great detail in her own book *An Omelette and a Glass of Wine*, published in 1984.

Australia's Gay Bilson served Conran another of his favourite meals at Bennelong, in Sydney, but he's blessed if he can remember what it was. 'I just remember it being really lovely and full of flavour. I also went to her restaurant at Berowra Waters on a sea plane and that was one of the best experiences ever, it was wonderful.'

Conran considers we are at an interesting crossroads in food. 'There are two directions. One way is the absolute passion that chefs have for getting Michelin stars and the over-decorated food that is necessary to gain them, and then there's the other way epitomized by [British chef] Fergie Henderson with terrific ingredients that are very simply cooked, not chefed. We've got this sort of divide between the guys that think they're artists and the guys who think they're craftsmen.' Conran leaves me in no doubt which of those directions he would always choose to follow.

'Unpretentious is my personal philosophy. We [he and his wife Vicki] called our book *Plain, Simple and Satisfying* and I suppose my abiding principle is loving the quality and flavour of the ingredients and wanting them put on the plate in a simple way. I don't disapprove at all of what [experimental chefs] Ferran Adria or Heston Blumenthal are doing. I'm enormously enthusiastic about people who are trying new things, it's what makes the world turn round, but if someone brings me a piece of meat with some potatoes and a good lettuce salad and a really good glass of burgundy I will be a happy man.'

'A great and glamorous way to eat rock oysters for those who don't like them raw. This dish is very filling, so we always allow four oysters per person as a starter, though some of our friends (and family) can eat six.'

oysters rockefeller

rock salt
500 g (1 lb 2 oz) spinach
75 g (2¹/₂ oz) butter
a splash of Pernod, or whatever pastis you have
1 teaspoon celery salt
a couple of dashes of Tabasco sauce
16 or 20 rock oysters (which, apart from being cheaper than natives, are available all year round)
100 g (3¹/₂ oz/1¹/₄ cups) fresh breadcrumbs

Put a layer of rock salt in a roasting tin large enough to take the oysters in a single layer.

Sweat the spinach, with only the moisture clinging to the leaves after washing, in a saucepan until it has wilted. Drain thoroughly, then put it in the bowl of a food processor with the butter, Pernod, celery salt and Tabasco, and whizz until you have a smooth green purée. Put it into the fridge to firm up.

Preheat the oven to 230° C (450° F/Gas 8).

Open the oysters, discarding the 'lid', and lay them in the roasting tin. The salt will keep them level.

When the spinach purée is firm, spread a spoonful over each oyster, using a palette knife to smooth them level. Sprinkle the breadcrumbs over the lot and place in the oven for 8–10 minutes, until the breadcrumbs have turned golden and the spinach purée has started to bubble around the edges.

Serve immediately, eating the oysters with a fork and taking care not to burn your fingers on the very hot shells.

Serves 4

terence conran

'This is best made towards the end of the season, with fresh peas that are just becoming slightly floury. In the winter months when fresh peas are not available, soaked split peas or frozen peas work well.'

pea and ham soup

50 g (1¾ oz) butter
1 onion, chopped
1 kg (2 lb 4 oz/6½ cups) shelled peas
1 litre (35 fl oz/4 cups) ham or gammon stock (or chicken stock)
100 g (3½ oz/⅔ cup) cooked ham or gammon, finely diced
salt and pepper
thick (double/heavy) cream, to serve

Melt the butter in a saucepan and sweat the onion until soft. Add the peas (or soaked split peas, or frozen peas) and turn them over in the butter for 1 minute.

Pour the stock into the pan and bring to a boil, then simmer for about 20 minutes until tender (split peas will need about 40 minutes).

Purée the soup in a blender, add the ham or gammon, then adjust the seasoning. Serve really hot, with a swirl of cream on top.

Serves 4

terence conran

braised beef with carrots

2 tablespoons dripping or oil
1.5 kg (3 lb 5 oz) braising beef
(rump or topside)
100 g (3½ oz) each of carrot, onion
and celery, finely sliced
1 calf's foot
1 bay leaf
1 sprig parsley
1 sprig thyme
500 ml (17 fl oz/2 cups) beef stock
or water/stock combination
400 g (14 oz) carrots, sliced
lengthways if large
salt and pepper
a splash of Madeira or port
a small handful of chopped flat-leaf
(Italian) parsley

Preheat the oven to 150° C (300°F/Gas 2).

Heat the dripping or oil in a large lidded casserole, add the beef and cook until brown and crusty on the outside. Spoon out most of the fat, then add the finely sliced vegetables, calf's foot, herbs and stock. Bring to a simmer on top of the stove. Cover, then transfer to the oven and braise for 1½ hours.

Meanwhile, cook the 400 g (14 oz) carrots in a pan of lightly salted boiling water for 10–15 minutes, until just tender. Drain well and keep warm.

Remove the beef from the casserole, cover and keep warm. Take the calf's foot out (delicious pickings for later). Skim the fat from the braising juices and strain through a conical sieve into a clean dish that you can bring to the table. Add salt, pepper and a splash of Madeira or port.

Slice the beef, return it and the boiled carrots to the serving dish and, making sure that it is really hot, serve sprinkled with some chopped parsley.

Plain boiled potatoes are an excellent accompaniment, as are young carrots or a green salad.

Serves 4

'There seems to be some argument as to whether this was a pudding invented by the college of the same name. It doesn't really matter how it came into being, it is one of the finest, and indeed most simple of puddings. You will need four 10–15 cm (4–6 inch) meringues; this recipe will make more than you need for Eton mess, but meringue keeps very well, wrapped in tissue paper, in a cake tin.'

eton mess

meringues
6 egg whites
a pinch of salt
a pinch of cream of tartar
350 g (12 oz) caster (superfine) sugar

500 g (1 lb 2 oz) strawberries, sliced
55 g (2 oz/¼ cup) vanilla sugar
500 ml (17 fl oz/2 cups) heavy (thick/double) cream, chilled
four 10–15 cm (4–6 inch) meringues, broken into pieces

For the meringues, preheat the oven to about 110° C (225° F/Gas ½). Line a large baking tray with non-stick baking (parchment) paper.

Beat the egg whites, salt and cream of tartar in a large bowl until the whites are stiff but not too dry and holey. While beating, allow 250 g (9 oz/1 cup) of the sugar to drift on to the whites and continue to beat until the mixture is stiff and glossy. Fold in the remaining sugar.

Place large spoonfuls of the meringue on the baking tray, making them round, oval or whatever shape takes your fancy. You can make a large pavlova if you want. Place the baking tray in the oven for 1 hour, then take a look and see if the meringues are sufficiently dry; if not, leave them for another 30 minutes.

Remove the meringues from the oven and transfer them to a wire rack to cool.

Place the strawberries in a glass or ceramic bowl and dredge with the vanilla sugar.

Pour the cream into the bowl in which you want to serve the pudding and beat it until it is lightly whipped.

Fold the strawberries and meringues into the cream — it should be faintly marbled. Serve immediately.

Serves 4

jill dupleix and terry durack

'Terry's slow food and I'm fast food', laughs Jill Dupleix. 'If we took the same cut of meat and some vegetables I'd have something on the table in ten minutes and he'd cook it for four hours. If we did something classic like *coq au vin*, he'd drive across town to get the right onions and angst about the wine, whereas I'd say "stuff the onions" and get it on the table within the hour. I cheat, he won't. I drive him crazy sometimes and he thinks I'm a kitchen harlot.'

Dupleix and Durack. Jill and Terry. Fast and slow. Both, of course, are independently successful food writers, who could easily have filled sections of this book on their own, but the times I have seen either of them alone over the years could probably be counted on one hand, so it seemed entirely appropriate to talk to them together.

In an interview in Melbourne's *The Age* newspaper, a journalist observed that the pair finish each other's sentences. They do, and each will often answer questions addressed to the other. Their creative synergy is extraordinary, despite Dupleix's claims that she and her husband are culinarily incompatible. 'He uses fifteen different knives, I tear things with my hands. He uses fat, I don't. His favourite ingredients include goose fat, salted pig's ears, chorizo and smoked eel. Mine include tomatoes, rocket, feta cheese, sashimi tuna and Campari. But we always love it when one cooks for the other.'

In 1999, when I moved to Australia, Jill Dupleix and Terry Durack were the undisputed power couple of the Sydney food scene, she as food editor of *The Sydney Morning Herald*, and he its restaurant critic. Together — and this was where their real influence lay — they edited the *Herald*'s *Good Food Guide*, the most feared of the city's several restaurant guides. The *Good Food Guide*, and Durack's weekly reviews, could make or break a restaurant. Their roles, especially in such a tight-knit community as Sydney, were by their very nature invidious ('our strategy was "we've got these great jobs, let's just do them to the best of our ability",' says Dupleix), but they had passion, integrity and the strength of their convictions and I believe the city's food scene is the poorer without them, now that they are based in London. When the pair withdrew a coveted 'chef's hat' (the *Good Food Guide*'s equivalent to a Michelin star) — as they did, famously, one year from Neil Perry's celebrated Rockpool — the sharp intake of breath could be heard in every Sydney restaurant.

The couple's influence was all the more remarkable given that neither is a Sydneysider. They're Melburnians who moved to Sydney in 1994. 'Melbourne people coming to Sydney to tell them how to eat and drink? That went over really well [the antipathy between the two cities is legendary], so it was hard work', recalls Durack. Then in 2000, they surprised the local industry by moving to the UK, Dupleix to take up the quaintly titled but influential position of 'Times Cook' at *The Times* and Durack to a newly created role as restaurant critic of *The Independent on Sunday*. Despite their new London identity, both retain strong links with Australia. Jill Dupleix's chatty, engaging cooking columns are a regular fixture in the original Australian edition of *ABC delicious.*, and she writes once again for *The Sydney Morning Herald*; Terry Durack's incisive restaurant reviews are reserved for his British readers, but his wry food musings appear in the *Herald*'s *Good Weekend* magazine.

They have been together for 25 years and married for 23. Both worked in advertising in Melbourne (Dupleix: 'I was a junior and he was a senior') and the shift to food journalism was gradual. As Dupleix explains, 'We discovered that we loved eating, drinking and cooking and we spent all our money on cooking classes around the world. As the years went on we were getting increasingly neurotic and unhappy in advertising but adored our other life. We just woke up one morning and said, "We love writing, we love food, why don't we write about food?".'

An entire bookshelf later (Dupleix has published thirteen books to Durack's six) their passion seems unflagging. Having edited them both — briefly and at different times — I can vouch they are an editor's dream, rarely requiring so much as a comma to be changed. 'I edit Jill and she edits me', says Durack. 'We agonize over every word.' Their office is currently their small apartment ('intimate' in real-estate parlance) slap bang in the middle of London's Notting Hill Gate. It's an enviable location whose only drawback would be the annual need to evacuate at Carnival time. 'We'd love to stay,' says Dupleix, almost apologetically, 'but it's so loud I have to pass a note to Terry saying "Would you like a cup of tea?".' Such is the economy of scale in the apartment that at the magic daily witching hour of Jill's 'Campari o'clock' (about 6 pm) the computers snap shut and the office converts to a dining room.

'Since moving to London our lives have been a total joy', says Durack. 'We haven't just shifted to England, we've shifted to Europe. I love having Europe all around, just there at the end of our arms.' Both admit the move from Australia has been a learning curve, a major shift for Durack being the need to adapt, ironically, to a much smaller audience than he was writing for in Sydney, largely due to the prohibitive cost of eating out in Britain.

Dupleix's adjustment to northern-hemisphere recipe writing was obviously swift, as she garnered a Cookery Journalist of the Year award in 2002 from the not-easily-impressed British Guild of Food Writers. And Durack was the recipient of the prestigious 2005 Glenfiddich Restaurant Critic of the Year trophy. All power to them both, as such honours are, to be honest, rarely collected by non-Brits. 'I'm very happy being a little on the outside looking in', explains Dupleix. 'An Australian will always get that in Britain, but I feel I can do anything here and that's the most wonderful feeling.'

There's a hint of professional rivalry that is gentle but persistent, beating just beneath the surface of their conversation. It's doubtless productive, and almost inevitable given their careers, but there's affection too. Each is the other's greatest fan. For purposes of British administration, Durack is currently Mr Jill Dupleix. 'We're Cookery Editor-and-spouse', teases Dupleix. 'I travel as the spouse and the Customs guys cack themselves laughing', adds her husband, with slightly less amusement.

Australian prawns and tropical fruit ('fruit that's had sunshine on it') might eventually lure them back to their homeland, while sea bass and 'fantastic' potatoes will be powerful reasons to stay in Britain. Like ex-pats and natives alike, they find London an exhilarating but exorbitant city in which to live and work. Moving from their beloved Notting Hill is not an option. 'Why would you live in London if you had to live in out in Woop Woop and not be able to buy a beautiful sea bass?' ponders Dupleix.

jill dupleix

'Salmon is already rich enough without adding sauces, creams and mayonnaises. Instead, bathe it in a gentle, fragrant broth of Thai aromatics with a little kick of lime juice, and serve with steamed rice.'

salmon in a light, fragrant broth

four 150 g (5½ oz) salmon fillets
4 tablespoons Thai fish sauce
2 stems lemon grass, trimmed
2 red Asian shallots, peeled
1 small red chilli
150 g (5½ oz) oyster, shiitake or button mushrooms
100 g (3½ oz) baby spinach leaves
500 ml (17 fl oz/2 cups) chicken or vegetable stock
1 teaspoon white sugar
1 tablespoon vegetable oil
sea salt and pepper
1 tablespoon fresh lime juice

Cut the salmon into wide fingers, coat it in half the the fish sauce and set aside.

Peel the lemon grass and finely slice the white part. Finely slice the shallots, chilli and mushrooms. Wash the spinach and drain.

Heat the stock in a saucepan with the lemon grass, shallots, chilli, mushrooms and sugar, and simmer for 10 minutes.

In the meantime, heat the oil in a nonstick frying pan and sear the salmon, skin side down, for 3 minutes or until crisped. Turn and lightly sear the other side, leaving the inside pink. Season well.

Wilt the spinach in the hot broth for 10 seconds, remove with tongs and arrange in four warmed shallow soup bowls. Place the salmon on top.

Add the remaining fish sauce and the lime juice to the broth, and spoon it around the salmon. Serve with a bowl of rice on the side.

Serves 4

'Terry and I once had a leg of lamb ready for dinner, but we were too hungry to wait for it to cook properly, so we slashed it down to the bone, stuffed the slashes with herby, garlicky crumbs, and roasted it in half the time. The best part is carving it, when you slice right across the lamb and the meat falls in fingers, with crisp skin at one end, pink and juicy meat at the other. Serve with a sharply dressed green salad and potatoes roasted in the same pan.'

slashed roast lamb

3 tablespoons roughly chopped flat-leaf (Italian) parsley
2 anchovies, chopped
3 cloves garlic, crushed
2 tablespoons salted capers, rinsed
1 tablespoon coarsely grated lemon zest
80 g (2³/₄ oz/1 cup) soft fresh breadcrumbs
3 tablespoons extra virgin olive oil, plus extra to drizzle
1 leg of lamb, about 2 kg (4 lb 8 oz)
4 sprigs rosemary or thyme
baby rocket (arugula) or spinach leaves
1 lemon, quartered

Heat the oven to 220° C (425° F/Gas 7). Combine the parsley, anchovies, garlic, capers, lemon zest and breadcrumbs in a bowl. Add the olive oil and squish the mixture into a soft, mushy paste.

Holding the leg of lamb with its meatiest side towards you, cut right down through the meat almost to the bone, at finger-width intervals. Push the stuffing down between the lamb 'slices', re-shape the meat and tie with string.

Scatter with rosemary or thyme, drizzle with a little olive oil and roast for 20 minutes. Reduce the heat to 190° C (375° F/Gas 5) and roast for 1 hour. Leave to rest under foil for 10 minutes.

Strain the juices into a bowl, and spoon off any surface fat. Remove the string and thickly carve across the lamb, parallel to the bone, forming chunky fingers of lamb.

Arrange loosely on warm plates, drizzle with the juices and scatter with baby rocket or spinach leaves. Serve with lemon wedges.

Serves 4–6

jill dupleix

'This is not so much a recipe as an idea, one that can be used time and again with summer's plums, peaches and apricots. Serve with crème fraîche or yoghurt as a dessert, or as part of a weekend brunch.'

simple plum tarts

4 firm, ripe plums
500 g (1 lb 2 oz) ready-rolled puff pastry
1 egg, beaten
1 tablespoon sugar
1 tablespoon butter
1 tablespoon honey or plum jam

Heat the oven to 200° C (400° F/Gas 6). Cut each plum in half so that you have eight 'cheeks', discarding the central stone.

Roll out the pastry if need be. To get the right size pastry bases, place a plum cheek on the pastry and trace a circle around it of 8–9 cm ($3^1/_4$–$3^1/_2$ inches) diameter, allowing a border of 1–2 cm ($^1/_2$–$^3/_4$ inches) around the fruit. Cut out eight circles, and arrange on lightly oiled baking sheets.

Brush each pastry circle with beaten egg and place a plum cheek, cut side down, on top. Scatter with the sugar, and dot with butter. Bake for around 20 minutes, until the plum is soft and the pastry is risen and lightly scorched. Drizzle a little honey or diluted plum jam over the top. Serve warm or at room temperature.

Makes 8

jill dupleix

'The extraordinary thing about red-cooking is that you're not just making red-cooked chicken, you're also making a master stock that has the ability to outlive you. Like a sourdough starter or a ginger beer mother, the master stock just keeps getting richer and better as it goes along, although once it has been used to cook fish, its glory days are over. If you either freeze it after use, or refrigerate it and remember to bring it to the boil every three days, it will keep indefinitely.'

chinese red-cooked chicken

125 ml (4 fl oz/½ cup) Chinese rice wine
1 tablespoon sugar
2 cloves garlic
2 cinnamon sticks
3 star anise
a large knob of ginger, peeled and sliced
125 ml (4 fl oz/½ cup) light soy sauce
125 ml (4 fl oz/½ cup) dark soy sauce
750 ml (26 fl oz/3 cups) chicken stock or water
1 teaspoon sesame oil, plus extra for rubbing
4 chicken marylands (leg quarters)
2 spring onions (scallions), finely sliced
steamed rice, to serve

Heat the rice wine and the sugar together in a large saucepan, stirring until the sugar dissolves. Add the garlic, cinnamon, star anise, ginger, light and dark soy, stock and sesame oil. Add the chicken pieces. They should fit quite snugly. If the liquid doesn't completely cover the chicken, add a little water, and a little extra soy if the colour starts to lighten.

Bring the liquid to the boil, skim off any froth, and reduce the heat to a very slow simmer, with the bubbles barely breaking the surface. Partly cover the saucepan, and gently simmer for 15–20 minutes. Turn the heat off and let the chicken steep in the liquid for at least 30 minutes, or until cool.

To serve, drain the chicken and rub with sesame oil. Chop the chicken through the bone Chinese-style into 1.5 cm (⅝ inch) sections, or discard the bones and slice the meat finely. Serve warm or at room temperature, with steamed rice and a little of the strained stock. Scatter with the spring onions.

Serves 4

terry durack

Opposite: chinese red-cooked chicken
Above: chorizo, squid and beans

'A warm salad linked by smoky Spanish paprika from the chorizo itself to the flour dusting on the squid. Serve with a dollop of good mayonnaise beaten with crushed garlic and more paprika.'

chorizo, squid and beans

4 fresh chorizo sausages
800 g (1 lb 12 oz) canned white beans (such as cannellini)
1 tablespoon olive oil
100 ml (3½ fl oz) chicken stock
1 teaspoon smoked paprika
1 cup (125 g/4½ oz) plain (all-purpose) flour
1 teaspoon salt
½ teaspoon pepper
1 teaspoon smoked paprika
500 g (1 lb 2 oz) fresh squid, cleaned
3 tablespoons light olive oil
100 g (3½ oz) baby rocket (arugula) leaves
1 lemon, quartered

Slice the chorizo sausages thickly, on the diagonal. Drain the beans and rinse. Fry the chorizo in olive oil in a frying pan until they crisp a little on the edges. Add the beans, chicken stock and paprika, and simmer gently for 5 minutes.

Mix the flour, salt, pepper and paprika together, and have ready a colander set over a basin. Cut the squid bodies into 1 cm (½ inch) rings, and the tentacles into smaller sections. Toss half the squid pieces in the flour, then tip them into the colander and vigorously shake off the excess flour into the bowl below. Heat half the light olive oil in a frying pan until hot, and fry the squid very quickly, turning once, then drain. Flour, shake and fry the remaining squid in the remaining light olive oil.

Divide the beans and sausage among four warmed dinner plates, scatter with rocket leaves and arrange the fried squid on top. Serve with lemon wedges.

Serves 4

terry durack

'Based on a classic Apulian recipe, this simple but satisfying pasta dish combines the inherent cuteness of orrecchiete (little ears) with the salty tang of anchovy and the satisfying crunch of fried breadcrumbs. Originally breadcrumbs were used as an economical substitute for cheese, but feel free to be recklessly extravagant, and to add some grated pecorino or parmigiano as well.'

orecchiette with cauliflower and anchovy

500 g (1 lb 2 oz) cauliflower
400 g (14 oz) orecchiette or penne
4 tablespoons olive oil
50 g (1³/₄ oz/¹/₂ cup) dried breadcrumbs or Japanese *panko* crumbs
8 Spanish anchovy fillets
1 clove garlic, finely sliced
¹/₂ red chilli, finely diced
freshly ground pepper

Bring a large pot of salted water to the boil. Cut the cauliflower into small florets and simmer until almost cooked, about 4 minutes. Remove the cauliflower with a slotted spoon. Bring the water back to the boil, add the pasta and cook until tender but still firm to the bite. Drain the pasta, reserving a cupful of the cooking water.

In a frying pan, heat 2 tablespoons of the olive oil, add the breadcrumbs and fry until golden, tossing well. Remove and set aside.

Clean out the frying pan and heat the remaining olive oil (mixed with a little anchovy oil if you like). Mash the anchovies roughly with a fork. Gently cook the anchovies, garlic and chilli until the anchovy has all but melted.

Add the cauliflower and stir through. Add the drained pasta and 3–4 tablespoons of the pasta water, tossing well. Add a generous amount of pepper and serve.

Serves 4

cherry ripe

Imagine the scene. Cherry Ripe, food writer and author, is telling me about the Cordon Bleu cookery course in which she enrolled in London in the early 1980s. Affecting her best Cordon Bleu-cum-Sloane Ranger-cum-1950s newsreader voice (the type that says 'yah' instead of 'yes'), she is holding an imaginary telephone to her ear. 'I said, "How do I tell if I'm advanced or intermediate?". They said, "Well, do you peel your tomatoes?". I said, "Yes of course, even cherry tomatoes." They were quite impressed with that. Then they said, "Well, can you make an emulsion sauce?" and I said, "Only a béarnaise, a choron or a hollandaise." They said, "You're advanced." '

I relay the story because it says two things about Cherry Ripe. One, she's a gifted — and very funny — storyteller. Two, she has quite obviously always been a stickler for detail. One can imagine the baby Cherry Ripe demanding to know the exact provenance of her Vegemite soldiers and their approximate gluten content. Strangely enough, Ripe admits that childhood mealtimes often revolved around 'discussion of what was on the plate, such as whether the pheasant could have been hung for longer'. So maybe not Vegemite.

Of course, there was no baby Cherry Ripe in the literal sense either. She was born Julitha Dent (Julitha is a Western Australian Aboriginal name) in Ludlow, Shropshire, in that beautiful region where England meets Wales. Her father was English, her mother Australian. Ripe moved to Australia when she was 12 and recalls she hated it. 'I arrived with red hair, lily-white skin and this strange Herefordshire accent, while all the posh private school girls had just come back from their summers at Palm Beach [on Sydney's northern beaches] with tanned legs and bronzed bodies. I felt like an outsider, added to which the trees didn't lose their leaves and there didn't appear to be any seasons. I really didn't like Australia at all.'

These days, Cherry Ripe is very proud to call Australia home (she once told me she considered Sydney the greatest city in the world) but there was some early toing and froing. In London, she worked as a rock journalist on the legendary *NME* with a pre-Pretenders Chrissie Hynde, and back in Australia, she was a rock columnist for *The Australian* and the *Sunday Telegraph*. Her food 'epiphany' came after interviewing chef Giorgio Locatelli, who 'created fake dog turds out of dried chocolate mousse' — amongst other unmentionables — for the cult 1990 movie *The Cook, The Thief, His Wife and Her Lover*. 'I took the article to *The Australian* who said "It's too stomach-churning for us but why don't you come and write about food?" ' So she did, and stayed 13 years.

There are two popular misconceptions about Cherry Ripe's name. One is that she changed her name by deed poll (she never has) and the other is that she named herself after the iconic Aussie chocolate bar. Well, that was only true until she discovered there was an Australian line of pedigree female Hereford called Cherry Ripe. 'So now I go with the cow.'

The name dates back to 1973, when Ripe was one of just two women in an 'outrageous and confronting' drag theatre group called Sylvia and The Synthetics. Distressed at being photographed in the group for *The Australian* newspaper and realising that her mother (who obviously knew nothing about this subversive side of

her daughter's life) was a reader, Ripe quickly came up with her new name for the photo caption. 'It was a toss-up between Cherry Ripe and Juicy Fruit.' In the light of her subsequent career, it was a fortuitous choice. One wonders if the illustrious and learned Oxford Symposium (which she has addressed on several occasions) would have invited Juicy Fruit to take the stand.

I met Cherry Ripe in London in 1998. I'd heard of her through her old friend Joan Campbell but had always assumed that Cherry Ripe was a nickname. So I was surprised to answer the phone to a strangely clipped Australian accent announcing that she was Cherry Ripe, that she would like to write for *Food Illustrated* and why didn't we do dinner?

Which is exactly what we did, and have continued to do on occasion ever since. But that first time, once my British reserve had adjusted to the shock of having every misspelling on the menu pointed out to the maitre d' before we'd even ordered a drink, we got on famously. And after a couple of bottles of wine we set about correcting the menus of every restaurant in Soho. What fun we had.

Cherry's one-and-only column in *Food Illustrated* appeared in March 1999 (my final issue as editor) and was a feisty diatribe on the deplorable condition of British restaurant fish. I loved it — and still do love the way Cherry Ripe writes — but the incoming editor obviously took a different view. Cherry was not invited back for a second attack.

Controversy has always been part of her armoury. In 1990, she wrote an article claiming Australians could eat better in Australia than in Europe, considered outrageous at the time by an audience still clinging to a cultural cringe (*Goodbye Culinary Cringe* was the title of Cherry Ripe's 1992 book), but she was almost certainly right. Her later claim that French food 'was dead' was considered blasphemy. 'You'd go to Paul Bocuse's restaurant and out would come a fish with pastry scales and you'd think "Why bother?" But you went to California in the early 90s and they'd stopped using butter and cream sauces,' Ripe explains. 'You could see that was going to be the way of the future.' Again, she was right.

Cherry Ripe is a passionate and forthright champion of Australian food culture and as such she was the ideal editor of the national newspaper's food pages. Though her weekly column was occasionally a rant, it was an incisive barometer of Australia's burgeoning food culture. 'I hope I, in some small part, encouraged Australians to be more confident about what they were doing and to realise that what we have here is as good as, and in many cases better than, what they have in Europe. I am opinionated and I don't back down from my opinions, but if I hold an opinion I hold it honestly.'

Ripe is dismissive of modern food editors 'who think there are two "t"s in frites and one "a" in béarnaise' (misspelling is a particular *bête noire*) and finds much modern food journalism depressing. 'Editors don't want to tackle the big issues anymore, like what we're doing to the environment and how our food is produced. They just want fluff, food as fashion and chefs as stars. It makes me very angry.'

When I suggest that fellow Australians Donna Hay and Bill Granger are currently the best-known envoys of this country's food overseas, I fear their gentler approach might be dismissed. But not a bit of it. Suddenly Cherry Ripe is all fluff herself. 'They both capture our light and our simplicity, and there's a lovely freshness about them. And if they get people in England going out and looking for really good-quality bread and eggs then I don't have any objection.'

I do believe she's mellowing.

'Chickpeas come in two types: desi, the smaller ones, and kabuli, the larger ones which I prefer. Do not be tempted to use canned chickpeas for this: they've lost their lovely nutty flavour, and are soaked in some awful goo. The celery gives the salad crunch, and the chorizo adds extra piquancy. For a vegetarian dish, leave out the sausage. Additional dressing with lemon-flavoured olive oil adds an extra dimension.'

chickpea salad

4 tablespoons finely diced celery heart
4 tablespoons lemon juice, or more to taste
400 g (14 oz) cooked chickpeas, cooled
16 slices of chorizo, lightly fried until crisp then sliced into strips
2 tablespoons finely diced red onion or shallot
ground black pepper, to taste
2 tablespoons finely chopped flat-leaf (Italian) parsley
1 tablespoon lemon-flavoured olive oil (optional)

Combine the celery and lemon juice in a non-metallic bowl and leave to steep.

Toss together the chickpeas, celery and lemon juice, chorizo and onion. Finally add black pepper and sprinkle with chopped parsley. For a richer finish, stir through the lemon-flavoured olive oil.

Serves 4

'You can now find boned duck breasts at farmers' markets. Otherwise, ask your butcher to bone out the breasts of two very plump European ducks such as Muscovy. The breasts should be 5–6 cm (2–2¹/₂ inches) thick. The rest of the carcasses can be made into a stew such as a coq au vin, *or a* confit.*'*

warm duck breast salad with crackling croutons

750 g (1 lb 10 oz) waxy potatoes
such as kipfler or pink fir apple
4 large boneless duck breasts
sea salt
salad greens, such as frisée
or escarole
walnut oil vinaigrette

Boil the potatoes until just tender when pierced with a skewer. Set aside to cool, then peel and slice into rounds.

Remove the skin from the duck breasts with a boning knife. Slice the skin into thin julienne strips, and then into fine dice.

In a large skillet or frying pan (preferably non-stick), very gently sauté the diced skin until it has released all its fat and has turned crisp and golden brown. With a slotted spoon, remove the duck-skin croutons from the rendered fat, retaining the fat. Place the croutons on paper towels to drain and sparingly sprinkle with good salt.

Turn up the heat under the frying pan to medium, and fry the duck breasts for about 5 minutes per side, until their outsides are browned, but their insides are still rare. (As with steak, the breasts should be tender when pressed. You can make an incision in one to check it's not too 'bleu'.) Remove the breasts from the pan and set aside to rest on a warm plate.

Strain the fat through a fine sieve to remove any sediment. Wipe the pan, return to it the clear, strained duck fat, and gently sauté the potatoes until golden brown and crisp on both sides. (Depending on the size of the pan you may need to do this in batches, as the potatoes need to be in a single layer.) It is important never to let the fat burn, and to remove all the sediment from the pan before adding the potatoes, otherwise you end up with burnt black bits. Slice the duck breasts into rounds, and fan on individual warmed plates.

Serve with the sautéed potatoes, and a green salad dressed with a walnut oil vinaigrette and sprinkled with the duck-skin croutons.

Serves 4

cherry ripe

'For this Vietnamese soup, I buy a whole roasted Peking-style Chinese duck. Once you have made this the first time, you can make a stock out of the carcass for the next time. It is important to have the most flavourful stock base possible.'

duck pho

1 Chinese roasted duck
1 litre (35 fl oz/4 cups) duck stock, de-fatted (put it in the fridge overnight, then skim off the fat)
2 star anise
250 g (9 oz) vermicelli rice noodles
1 small bunch coriander (cilantro)
1 small bunch saw-toothed coriander (culantro/*rau mui tau*)
1 small bunch Vietnamese mint (*rau ram*)
1 small bunch sweet mint (*rau thom*)
1 small bunch holy basil
500 g (1 lb 2 oz) fresh bean sprouts
1 small butter lettuce, torn into small pieces
4 spring onions (scallions), sliced into 3 cm (1¼ inch) lengths
2 tablespoons fried shallots (available in Asian grocers)
50 g (1¾ oz/⅓ cup) roasted peanuts, chopped

condiments
1 lime, cut into 8 wedges
1 red chilli, finely sliced, placed in a small bowl with Thai fish sauce to cover
chilli jam
prawn crackers, optional

Preferably wearing rubber gloves, bone the duck, separating the skin, transferring the lean meat to a bowl and putting the carcass in a stock pot for the next time. (Discard the 'parson's nose,' as it can impart an unpleasant flavour.)

Put the stock and star anise in a saucepan, bring to the boil, cover to prevent evaporation, then keep at a bare simmer until ready to serve.

On a chopping board, scrape as much fat as possible from the duck skin, place the pieces of skin in a single layer between paper towels and blast for a few seconds in the microwave, being careful not to burn the skin. Squeeze out the fat, discard the paper towel and repeat with clean paper towel until you have fat-free crackling. Slice this into julienne and put in a bowl.

Shred the lean meat into small pieces large enough to pick up with chopsticks, place in a bowl and set aside. Soak the rice noodles in boiling water, drain, place in a bowl and set aside. De-stalk the herbs and tear the leaves into small pieces for garnish.

Put each ingredient in a separate bowl in an assembly line in the order in which they will go into the individual large soup bowls.

To serve, in each warmed soup bowl, first place an equal amount of the rice noodles, then the bean sprouts, duck meat, lettuce, spring onion and herbs. Remove the star anise from the broth then ladle the broth over the top and garnish with duck skin, crumbled fried shallots and chopped peanuts.

Serve with chopsticks and soup spoons, preferably Chinese-style ones. Place the condiments on the table for diners to help themselves. For extra texture, I also like to serve prawn crackers; they can be crisped in the microwave on a medium setting for 30 seconds.

Serves 4

'Buy the strongest-scented strawberries and raspberries you can find. While it's preferable to use leaf gelatine, as it's so much more pure, it's hard to give precise quantities for it. The quantity given here is for powdered gelatine. Using frozen fruit for this recipe is not recommended, as it goes too mushy.'

summer berry jelly

500 g (1 lb 2 oz) ripe strawberries
500 g (1 lb 2 oz) mixed berries
(such as raspberries, red currants,
black currants and/or blueberries)
2 tablespoons sugar, or sweetener
to taste
200 ml (7 fl oz) water
juice of 2 blood oranges or tangelos
10 grams ($^1/_4$ oz) powdered gelatine
mascarpone or crème fraîche,
to serve

Wash and hull the strawberries and cut them into quarters. Pick over the berries and remove all the stalks from the currants.

In a saucepan, make a syrup of the sugar and water. Add half the strawberries and poach gently until soft. With an immersion blender, purée the mixture. Add the citrus juice, reduce the heat to low then add the gelatine and stir to dissolve it. Do not boil the mixture, as this can prevent the gelatine from setting. Purée again to remove any lumps.

Put the remaining strawberries and the mixed berries in the serving bowl (preferably clear glass, unless you are going to turn it out) and pour the hot syrup over the fruit. Put the bowl in the fridge to set. On a hot day, leave it in the fridge until nearly ready to serve. Serve with mascarpone or crème fraîche.

Serves 6

cherry ripe

kevin gould

In the mid-1990s, in London, if your party wasn't catered by Kevin Gould it just wasn't happening. When Gould tells you he had to turn down David Bowie because he was booked by Tony Blair the same night he's certainly not joking, nor is he bragging, because at the time that was really how it was. He was the 'real-food' guru, a foodie rock star when Jamie was barely out of short pants. Clients would pay a small fortune for Gould's pistachio nuts thrown artfully across bare tables, milky white clouds of organic *mozzarella di bufala* and olives the size of quail's eggs, flown in from Marseilles. When Kevin Gould came to the party there were shot glasses of *affogato* and a man standing by with cleansing rosewater. Ab Fab? Absolutely (in fact, British PR supremo Lynne Franks, the genesis of Eddie Monsoon in the television series, was a client), but Kevin Gould was something of a cult himself long before Eddie and Patsy.

kevin gould

Kevin Gould and I met around 1997, when I was asked to write about him for the *Saturday Express Magazine*. Gould was throwing a dinner party for the Express cameras at Joy, his delicatessen, in Hampstead, north London. I'd heard a bit about him and I had one or two friends who were devotees of his Real Food store, in trendy Maida Vale, but when we met I remember being struck by Kevin Gould's quite obvious passion for his food and — unusually for then — his preoccupation with the provenance of ingredients. Gould was a wonderful storyteller, a real old-fashioned raconteur, and I remember thinking that if he could write even half as well as he could talk, he'd make a damn good columnist. Nobody had ever said that to him before and I'm glad I got in first.

Kevin Gould's column appeared in the first issue of *Food Illustrated* in March 1998 and he has rarely missed an issue since. That first column, celebrating Easter food on the Greek islands, was quite barmy but totally engaging, and teamed with Trevor Flynn's abstract illustration it added just the right note of eccentricity. The formula has never really changed.

Over lunch in October 2004, at Gould's favourite Lindsay House restaurant in Soho, that engaging passion is quick to resurface. Having offloaded his catering company and closed the delis several years ago ('I remember waking up one morning and realizing that I owed a million quid'), Gould now writes full time. He's written several books with such titles as *Dishy* and *Loving and Cooking with Reckless Abandon*. When we met, a third volume, with the bizarre (but infuriatingly on-the-money) title of *Kitchen Yoga*, was on the Gould back burner. 'The joy now', he says, 'is that I get plenty of time to think. Maybe I'm earning less money but so what, I feel kind of richer for it.'

'I'm not on any great mission to educate but at the same time I think you get more pleasure out of what you eat if you know where it's from.' As I fiddle with my tape recorder, he's away on the stream-of-consciousness roll that I remember well, something about Ryvita crispbread — which is apparently ice bread ('dough, salt and water with the shit beaten out of it at a very cold temperature') — and some cunning Finns hiding the sourdough starter in the forest when their country was invaded by the Russians. By the time I've got my tape running smoothly, we're in Darjeeling (the downside of being Kevin Gould is apparently that 'it's sometimes hard to have just a cup of tea') and then we're off to Louisiana on the hunt for a rare chipotle sauce by way of the Singha beer brewery in Thailand. And all this before our drinks have even arrived.

Gould's own heritage is colourful, born in Manchester, in the north of England, from mixed Russian, German, Jewish, Egyptian and Syrian stock. As he tells it, 'My father's grandfather was a Cossack rider in the circus, my grandfather was in the music halls and my father went into cling-film.' Gould feels he inherited his food genes (his own foray into cling-film didn't work out and he went off to learn how to cook in France) from his Syrian grandmother, who 'at any time of the day or night had to be able to provide food for no matter how many people, as that was the Syrian way'.

'I remember the smell of the kitchen even now. From the age of five I thought this was how everyone ate. Friday night was the big one when the whole family got together. There'd be thirty people around the table, at least five types of rice and who knows how many fried fish and baked meats. It was only later on at school when I'd go to someone else's house for tinned strawberries [Gould grew up in the sixties] and Fray Bentos pies that I thought "Hang on, how have we been living here?".'

Generosity and boundary pushing have always been his signatures, as evident these days in the writing as they once were in the food. Shortly before I moved to Australia, Gould opened a café called Love at the Aveda store in London's chic Marylebone High Street. I remember the fresh bread loaves, stuffed full of caramelized shallots and roasted garlic, placed communally, the idea being that customers just tore chunks off and helped themselves. Nice idea apart from the fact that when the customer left, the bread remained, ready for the next hungry paw. Gould's inspiration was 'fertilization around the table', breaking down barriers by 'tearing a piece of bread and offering it to the stranger next to you.' Not surprisingly, the hygiene lobby was unimpressed, fearing that something a lot more sinister might be spread around the table, and the loaves disappeared.

Kevin Gould will always walk on the wild side of food. 'If you can eat together, then you can get rid of a lot of your differences,' he says, citing a wonderfully mad, Heath Robinson moment which summons all one's powers of visualization. At a party for the Institute of British Architects, Gould 'arranged stainless steel guttering from a big platform in the corner of the room, on a slight decline. We buttered it with ghee and had a stainless steel cement mixer [procured by Sir Richard Rogers] that could actually heat things up. We had all the architects sitting at long tables and put beautiful food down the middle — prosciutto, fantastic olives and caperberries and cheese — and we made polenta in the cement mixer and let it slide down the guttering like a river.'

If anyone else told me this story, I might feign amusement and dismiss it as nonsense. But when Kevin Gould tells it, you know he's probably playing it down. The reality would have been even crazier.

'I love the idea of old colonial types called Bufton Tufton and Rolly knocking back medicinal pink gins. The only gin I've come to love is Martin Miller's 40 per cent proof Westbourne Strength, distilled in Birmingham, England, then sent to Borganes, Iceland, to be mixed down to strength with the cleanest, most refreshing water imaginable.'

pink gin

gin
bitters — Trinidadian Angostura, for preference, or Peychauds, from New Orleans
candied angelica, to garnish

Make ice cubes by putting 5 drops of bitters in each compartment of an ice-cube tray, and filling up with water. Freeze.

Put 3 or 4 cubes in a frozen old-fashioned glass and add a good slug of gin. Garnish with a thin sliver of bright green candied angelica as a swizzle stick.

If you wish, you can rim each glass beforehand with preserving sugar (bigger crystals, you see) that you've coloured up with a few splashes of bitters.

kevin gould

'These "cherry Marys" make thought-provoking, mouth-exploding canapés, and are fine sharpeners when served at a Sunday brunch. You will be able to tell a great deal about your guests by the manner in which they eat these whole-food cocktails. Those who pop them immediately, unquestioningly, straight into their mouths and are exhilarated by the dish will generally make more spontaneous lovers than timorous nibblers.

For this recipe, you will need a hypodermic syringe. These are easy enough to buy from most pharmacies. Ten-millilitre syringes are sold over the counter, but it is better to have a larger syringe if possible. Ask the pharmacist nicely and explain that all you're addicted to is good living. Make sure that whichever syringe you score has the largest possible diameter needle, as the spicy mixture can gum up the works.'

tomatoes with a love injection

12 perfect cherry tomatoes, brought up to room temperature for at least an hour
200 ml (7 fl oz) good-quality vodka
1 tablespoon worcestershire sauce
1 teaspoon red or green Tabasco sauce
a good pinch of salt, dissolved in the juice of half a lemon

With an empty syringe, enter each tomato through its green head and remove as much juice as you are able. Keep the juice, if you like, to add to any soup or stock that you might be making.

Mix all the wet ingredients and stir them very well. Drain the mixture through muslin or a double thickness of kitchen paper.

Fill the syringe with the filtered liquid and tap it a couple of times in order to remove any air bubbles and appear professional.

Inject a small amount through the green head into each tomato. Take care, though; inject too much, and the skin will split — you'll need less than you think.

Chill, if you have the time, for an hour or so, before your guests arrive.

Serve with small napkins, as the tomatoes can spurt alarmingly.

Makes 12

kevin gould

'Koushary is Egyptian street food, working food and a great leveller. Old Cairo has numerous koushary shops. Brightly lit window displays of man-sized mounds of rice, chickpeas and spicy tomato sauce tempt passers-by from all walks of life to a fuel stop. The koushary version of rice, where it is cooked with macaroni, confuses Western sensibilities by mixing two starches in the same dish, but is a satisfying contrast of tastes and textures. Too much koushary may make you walk like an Egyptian, but no dish better illustrates the Egyptian paradox, where pasta is cooked with rice, where the future is behind them and the past continues to happen. This recipe is a (somewhat refined) version of the rice served in koushary shops. It demonstrates rice to be the easy, tasty convenience food that it is for more than half the world.'

koushary

light vegetable oil, for frying
1 nest of vermicelli
500 g (1 lb 2 oz) basmati rice, in a measuring jug
1½ times the volume of rice in boiling water
sea salt
butter, optional

In a heavy-bottomed lidded pan, over a high heat, heat the oil and add the vermicelli, stirring. The vermicelli will go brown in a few seconds. As soon as it does, throw in the rice. Stir for 1 minute, until every grain has a coating of oil.

Add all of the water and bring back to the boil. Add salt to taste, stir again and put the lid on firmly.

Reduce the heat to very low and cook, undisturbed, for about 20 minutes (the time will vary slightly depending on the age and quality of the rice you use).

Take the rice off the heat and run a fork through it, to separate the grains further. Some people like to run lots of butter through the rice at this point. I'm one of them.

Allow the rice to rest, lid on, for about 15 minutes before serving.

Serves 4

'Haçik Keshishian, an Armenian who once owned a kebab shop in London's Camden Town, was the master of the massaged shoulder. "Shoulder!" he would say, pointing to his own broad, brawny specimen for emphasis, "that's where the bloodyhell best flavour is!". He would demonstrate that this cheap cut of lamb needs special attention if it is to achieve its full flavour potential. "Relax the meat. Make it very ready for you, take the flavourings, and push and rub, like this." His concentration was absolute; communing is not too loaded a word to describe the affectionate attention he would pay to his ingredients.

This recipe is inspired by and is dedicated to the fond memory of Haçik Keshishian, who died in 1992, having served so many people such heavenly food.'

massaged shoulder of lamb

2 cloves garlic
One 2 kg (4 lb 8 oz) shoulder
of lamb, boned out
1 bunch mint
juice of 1 lemon
olive oil
black pepper
1 tablespoon white wine vinegar

Preheat the oven to 230° C (450° F/Gas 8). Slice the garlic cloves in two and rub the meat all over with the cut ends. Roughly chop the mint, moisten it with lemon juice and olive oil and grind a few turns of the pepper mill over it.

Lay the meat fat side up. Slowly and methodically, start to massage the aromatic mint mixture into the meat with your fingertips. Allow at least 10 minutes for this and allow your own stresses to disappear with your kneading and pinching movements. Turn the meat over, and repeat the massage, re-moistening the mixture as needed.

Spread the minty mixture all over the joint, then roll it lengthways. With cut pieces of trussing string, secure the joint with four slip knots, then link the slip knots together top and bottom with a continuous length of string, and tie off.

Place the joint on a rack in a roasting tin containing a cup of water in the preheated oven. Immediately reduce the heat to 220° C (425° F/ Gas 7) and roast for 30 minutes. Baste well with the pan juices, turn the joint over and reduce the heat to 180° C (350° F/Gas 4). If the juices in the roasting pan are burning, add a further cup or so of hot water to them. Roast for about 1 hour, remove from the oven and let the joint rest, loosely covered in foil, for 15 minutes.

Using a double layer of kitchen paper, skim the fat off the pan, then deglaze the pan with the vinegar. Pour the juices into a saucepan and heat so that the mixture bubbles and reduces. Remove the string from the joint and serve it sliced, with its juices.

Serves 4

It would have been 1996 or 1997. The Australian food writer Cherry Ripe was my dining partner that night and she wouldn't let me leave Sydney's Darley Street Thai restaurant until I had met its chef patron, David Thompson. Cherry can be very persuasive and, weakened by the ravages of jet-lag (I had flown in from the UK the day before) but happily sated by the most incredible Thai meal I had ever eaten, I gave in.

david thompson

We sat patiently in the lipstick-pink dining room, ordered more wine and waited. At the end of service, the perspiring chef timidly appeared clutching a stack of old manuscripts sealed in plastic bags. These, I learned, were just a few of the hundreds of antique Thai cookbooks and memorial books in Thompson's personal collection, exquisite documents — some of which dated back to the 1920s and 1930s — that have inspired and instructed him in his exhaustive, scholarly study of Thai cooking. I was enthralled by the memorial books that celebrated the lives of well-born Thais, prepared by their families as part of the traditional funeral rites. In the case of women, these books frequently contained the recipes they had cooked over a lifetime, recipes handed down through the generations. On that first meeting, I knew little about Thompson other than that he cooked magical food that bore no resemblance to the Thai food I had eaten in London, or indeed on any of my own visits to Thailand. I realised this was a man of extraordinary talent with a very singular passion. And a dry wit that can catch you unawares.

Fast-forward to October 2004, and Thompson and I are chatting over lunch in London at nahm, the restaurant he opened in 2001 in Mayfair's Halkin Hotel, and to which he is now a consultant. We've sampled the sweet, sour and salty complexity of *ma hor*, minced prawn and chicken simmered in palm sugar with deep-fried shallots, served on pineapple and mandarin, *neua pat nahm prik*, a spicy stir-fry of beef, and *geng gari gai*, an aromatic curry of chicken with pumpkin and cucumber relish. It's a different dining room on the opposite side of the world, but the flavours vividly recall that earlier night in Sydney's Kings Cross. Thompson has made his home in Britain, and while Australia misses him, London has embraced him. In 2002, nahm became the first Thai restaurant ever to be awarded a coveted Michelin star. I wanted to know where Thompson's affinity with Thailand began.

'It was a bloody accident', he recalls. 'I went to Thailand instead of Tahiti and just fell in love with the place. I was seduced by the country, the culture and its people. Thailand is the most agreeable place and for a little white boy from Sydney, what I found exciting was the edge of chaos on which most people lived. There was an energy and verve that was exotic and slightly dangerous.'

Trained in the classic French style ('French in that stupid Australian way where an avocado was the height of chic'), Thompson originally had no appetite for what passed as Thai food in Sydney in the 1980s, food he now dismisses as 'a clichéd, hackneyed adulteration of a remarkable culinary heritage' (interestingly, Thompson believes that the Thais' intrinsic willingness to please has led them to adulterate their own food for fear of offending Western palates). He remembers some 'despicable' Thai fish cakes in a Bondi restaurant, 'and this really strange herb called lemon grass which I found very disagreeable.'

Bangkok was a delicious epiphany. 'If the Thais are not eating food, it's because they are preparing food', he observes. 'And if they're not eating or preparing it, they're talking about it or shopping for it. Thai life is about food and despite the fact that they eat incessantly they don't get fat. There can be no god in heaven.'

He met his longstanding Thai partner, Tanongsak Yordwai, there. 'Through Tanongsak I met this old woman who introduced me to a different type of cooking. It was food from the palaces of Bangkok and it was gobsmackingly good.' The woman was Sombat Janphetchara, the wife of a high-ranking bureaucrat. 'I still remember the first dish of hers that I tasted, a sour orange curry of *pla chorn* (a meaty freshwater fish) that had been deep-fried then plunged into a curry with lots of tamarind, deep-fried chillies and whole red shallots. I can still see the dish, and I can still taste it. The clarity of her flavours, the definition of her textures and the deft way in which she seasoned could only have come about because of the inherited skills she possessed. I was overwhelmed.'

Thompson is an eloquent interviewee. He speaks quietly and quickly but chooses his words with precision to reflect his passion and reverence for his adopted cuisine. When I ask what he considers to be the appeal of Thai food, I anticipate the response might be a complex equation of flavour, texture and fragrance. 'It tastes bloody good, it's as simple as that. You can talk about its venerable history, you can talk about its fascinating techniques, you can be as cerebral as you like, but the proof of any cuisine is how it tastes.'

Thai Food, the lavish, Darley-Street-pink volume Thompson published in 2002, is regarded as the seminal English-language reference book on Thai cuisine. The author is a little vague as to exactly how long it took him to write, but my guess is about five years. He swears it started life as a book on Thai snacks that just grew and grew. 'You know how tremendously ill-disciplined cooks are', Thompson comments mischievously. 'I thought deadline was the time that you start and so I did absolutely nothing. And then Julie [Julie Gibbs, his publisher at Penguin Books in Australia] got a little frustrated two years after the deadline and I thought I'd better start.'

I suspect there's a grain — but only a grain — of truth in all that, but Thompson nevertheless produced a remarkable book that runs to almost 700 pages. It won him a slew of international awards, including a Glenfiddich Award in Britain, giving the lie to the occasionally-heard claim that the elite food publishing awards are never bestowed on non-Brits. 'Unlike most cooks,' he explains, 'who write books in order to make people go to their restaurants, I thought I might as well give them all the keys to unlock this cuisine, or at least all the keys I knew, and it just grew from there. It's heartening to realise that in spite of the current atmosphere of dumbing everything down there are still people who are interested in the authentic stuff.'

Thompson loves London and he's planning to stay, for the time being at least. London, even more than Sydney, allows him to really cook the food he loves to cook. Unlike in Australia, there are no restrictions on what he can import into Britain, and most of the fresh produce used at nahm is imported from Thailand. 'We have buyers in Bangkok who package everything and once a week we get a delivery of all our gingers, wild gingers, kaffir lime leaves, Thai basil. The quality is palpably, outstandingly, different and it allows us to do things we would otherwise be unable to do.'

'London is a place where once, if you were wise, you ate before you came', he says with mock solemnity. 'It's changed tremendously. There's something charming about this mouldy, smelly, frustrating, dank, dirty, crowded city. And in two hours you can be in Marseilles or in Austria. Where can you be in two hours from Sydney? Dubbo?'

salad of chicken and pomelo

dressing
dressing
2 coriander (cilantro) roots
1/2 large red chilli, de-seeded
a few small bird's eye chillies
a good pinch of salt
4 tablespoons lime juice
2 tablespoons white sugar
3 tablespoons Thai fish sauce

100 g (3½ oz) blanched and shredded
chicken
225 g (8 oz/1 cup) pomelo
segments, peeled
2 stems lemon grass, finely sliced
2 sliced red Asian shallots
handful of mint and coriander
(cilantro) leaves
deep-fried garlic (see note)
deep-fried shallots (see page 115)

Combine all the dressing ingredients in a mortar and pound with a pestle. The dressing should not be too strong, otherwise it will overwhelm the chicken and fruit, but nor should it be too weak: it should be salty, and equally sweet, sour and hot.

Combine with the remaining ingredients and serve sprinkled with the deep-fried garlic and shallots.

Serves 4 as part of a shared meal

Note: For garlic to deep-fry successfully, a certain amount needs to be fried — usually at least 1 cup — otherwise it is difficult to control the cooking, and it can burn easily and all too quickly. Slice the garlic lengthways into thin, even slices. It is important to slice it lengthways, so that the slices deep-fry evenly and crisply, rather than becoming knotted disks. The slices should also be as fine as possible, almost paper thin, so that they cook quickly and evenly and become crisp and golden; if they are too thick, the edges will burn while the inside remains undercooked.

Heat oil in a wok until moderately hot, then add the garlic and reduce the heat a little. Deep-fry, stirring constantly with tongs. When the garlic starts to lose its sharp peppery aroma and smells nutty, and starts to turn amber and then a light honey-gold, remove it from the oil. Drain and spread out on absorbent paper to cool. Pass the oil through a sieve to collect any scraps before re-use; the garlic-infused oil can be used for deep-frying or stir-frying.

The garlic will keep for 2–3 days in an airtight container.

sour orange curry
of prawns with betel leaves

chicken stock
chicken bones (or a whole chicken)
salt
ginger
garlic
offcuts of spring onions (scallions),
cabbage or coriander (cilantro)
stalks (depending on what
is at hand)
peeled daikon
shiitake mushroom stalks, optional

sour orange curry paste
4 tablespoons tamarind pulp,
any seeds removed
2 tablespoons purée of dried long
red chillies
a few bird's eye chillies
a good pinch of salt
3 tablespoons minced garlic
3 tablespoons ground dried shrimp
(ideally freshly made)
1 tablespoon shrimp paste (*gapi*)

5 red Asian shallots
1 tablespoon tamarind water,
optional (see notes)
a pinch white sugar
2 tablespoons Thai fish sauce
2 heaped tablespoons sour orange
curry paste (above)
6 cleaned raw prawns (shrimp)
a few torn 'betel' leaves
a pinch roasted chilli powder,
or to taste (see notes)
3 deep-fried dried long red chillies

To make the stock, blanch the rinsed bones from a cold-water start with a pinch of salt. Refresh and rinse once more. Crush them slightly with a pestle or heavy object, then cover with cold water, add salt and bring to the boil. Allow to simmer for 20 minutes, then add the vegetables. Continue to simmer for 2 hours, then strain.

To make the curry paste, using a pestle, pound each ingredient in a mortar, in the given order, until thoroughly puréed before adding the next ingredient. If using the tamarind pulp in the paste, then there is no need for the tamarind water to season the curry.

To make the curry, add a pinch of the salt to 3 cups of the stock and bring to the boil. Add the tamarind water (if using) and the shallots and simmer until tender. Season with sugar and fish sauce. Add the paste and simmer for a minute or so. Check the seasoning: this thin curry should taste salty, sour and hot. Add the prawns, betel leaves, chilli powder and deep-fried chillies and simmer just until the prawns turn pink.

Notes: To make tamarind water, break off an amount of pulp, rinse to remove any surface yeasts, then cover in a similar amount of warm water and leave for a few minutes to soften. Squeeze and work the pulp to dissolve, then strain to remove any fibres or seeds. It is best to make it quite thick, as this can always be diluted later; very thin tamarind water added to a curry, soup or relish may over-dilute it.

To make roasted chilli powder, roast 1 cup of dried bird's eye or dried long red chillies in a wok or pan over a medium heat, stirring regularly to prevent scorching, until they have changed colour and are beginning to toast. Cool, then grind to a coarse or fine powder, as preferred, in a pestle and mortar or a clean coffee grinder. The powder keeps well in an airtight container.

Serves 4 as part of a shared meal

Above: sour orange curry of prawns with betel leaves
Opposite: mangosteen, lychees and rambutans in perfumed syrup with green mango and deep-fried shallots

stir-fried bean sprouts with yellow beans, garlic and chillies

2 cloves garlic
a pinch of salt
1 long red chilli
vegetable oil, for frying
150 g (5¹/₂ oz) bean sprouts, topped
and tailed
3 tablespoons yellow bean sauce
a pinch of white sugar
125 ml (4 fl oz/¹/₂ cup) chicken stock
(see page 111)
2 tablespoons light soy sauce

Crush the garlic with the salt in a pestle and mortar. Add the chilli and bruise with the pestle.

Heat a wok, add the oil and then throw in the bean sprouts, crushed garlic, chilli, yellow bean sauce and sugar. When the bean sprouts are wilted, add the stock and light soy sauce. Serve immediately.

Serves 4 as part of a shared meal

david thompson

mangosteen, lychees and rambutans in perfumed syrup with green mango and deep-fried shallots

200 g (7 oz) white sugar
300 ml (10½ fl oz) water, ideally perfumed with a little jasmine or rose water
1 pandanus leaf, knotted
som saa zest
a little *som saa* juice
a good pinch of salt, perhaps even a teaspoon
jasmine flowers, optional (it is vital that they be organic)
10 mixed mangosteens, lychees and rambutans
a little crushed ice — perhaps perfumed with a little jasmine or rose water
1 tablespoon shredded green mango
3 tablespoons deep-fried shallots (see note)

Make a syrup by simmering the sugar and water, adding the pandanus leaf, *som saa* zest and salt. Just before removing from the heat, pour in the *som saa* juice. Simmer briefly, then remove from heat. Cool and strain. Add a few jasmine flowers, if available, to enhance the perfume.

Peel the fruit and prise out the seeds. Pour the cold syrup over the fruit, add crushed ice, the green mango and sprinkle with deep-fried shallots to serve.

Serves 4 as part of a shared meal

Note: Deep-fried shallots are an important garnish in Thai cooking. Although they can be bought in stores, it is much better to fry your own. You'll need to fry at least 1 cup of shallots at a time, in order to control their cooking; they can burn easily and all too quickly. It takes 2 cups of fresh red Asian shallots to make 1 cup of deep-fried.

Slice the shallots lengthways into very thin, even slices. Heat oil in a wok until moderately hot, then turn up the heat and add the shallots; be careful, as the oil will bubble up. When the oil has recovered its heat, reduce the heat slightly. Deep-fry, stirring constantly with tongs, until the shallots begin to colour. Make sure the oil remains quite hot throughout, otherwise the shallots will absorb oil and become soggy. Remember that the shallots will continue to cook for a few moments after they have been removed from the oil, so when they have lost their onion-like aroma and begin to smell enticingly nutty, are becoming golden and starting to stick to the tongs a little, drain and spread out on absorbent paper to cool. The shallots should crisp as they begin to cool, retaining surprisingly little oil. Pass the oil through a sieve to collect any scraps; the shallot-perfumed oil can be used for deep-frying or stir-frying.

The shallots will keep for 2 days in an airtight container.

sybil kapoor

I had made the hasty but not entirely illogical assumption that Sybil Kapoor was Indian, so when I walked into the café where we had agreed to meet in late 1997, Sybil Kapoor was the last person that I expected to be Sybil Kapoor. Quietly and precisely spoken, what my mother's generation might have described as *gamine*, Kapoor is unequivocally English, from the rural Surrey Downs in southern England. In fact, every inch the Sybil Polhill that she was before she married her husband Raju Kapoor, a consultant neurologist, some twenty-three years ago.

Sybil Kapoor wrote for *Food Illustrated* as a contributing food editor from its launch in March 1998. Her monthly recipes, which gently followed the rhythm of the seasons, became a focal point of the magazine. The cover of the very first issue bore the bold question 'What is British Food?' beneath an ethereal shot of Kapoor's violet almond chocolate profiteroles. With hindsight, the accompanying feature, with more 'modern British' recipes, David Loftus's magical photography, but a frustratingly brief text, belies Kapoor's knowledge of her subject. I believe she is the contemporary expert on British food, following in the wake of her own mentors, writers like Jane Grigson, the lesser-known Dorothy Hartley and Mrs Beeton's nineteenth-century precursor, Eliza Acton.

To borrow Tamasin Day-Lewis's phrase, Sybil Kapoor is a 'scholar cook'. It's a quaint term that suits her well. Chatting in the sitting room of her smart central London townhouse, I ask Kapoor if her strongly

intellectual approach defines her as a food historian. 'I think a historian is someone who really researches very deeply. I research well but I don't go reading old manuscripts. I think of myself as more contemporary than that. But I'm fascinated by food history, I love being able to give people a sense of what has actually gone before, a sense of continuity.'

In many respects, Kapoor too is an accidental foodie. At least, an accidental food writer. Her path to her profession — and certainly to her stance on British food — has been interestingly haphazard. An unhappy spell as a secretary led to her cooking directors' lunches in corporate dining rooms.

'I had a few disasters but I fell in love with cooking and realized that was the life for me.' She describes working for Justin de Blank at his small restaurant at London's Institute of Contemporary Art [Nigel Slater was also a de Blank 'graduate'] as her first 'proper job'. 'We made everything ourselves, the bread, the yoghurt, literally everything, and it was very civilized. We had coffee breaks and tea breaks — which I didn't realise was very atypical — and I thought "This is a lovely life!".'

Things were a little less civilized, but no less inspiring, a few years later when Kapoor and her husband moved temporarily to New York and she found herself working in the kitchen at Jams, a brave restaurant that served unfashionably robust Californian food to fashionable New Yorkers at the height of the nouvelle cuisine fad. Already a devotee of Alice Waters's pared-back style of cooking at Chez Panisse restaurant in Berkeley, California (Kapoor still cites Waters's *Chez Panisse Cookbook* as one of her enduring influences), she found it a revelation. 'It was free-form food and very beautiful', she recalls. 'They were reinterpreting American dishes using fantastic American produce and combining it with French sauces, amazing salads and mesquite grills. Woody Allen and Jackie Onassis would come in and pay vast amounts of money for the most perfectly-made French fries with a mesquite grilled steak and red wine sauce.'

Back in England, Kapoor worked for chef Sally Clarke at her respected eponymous restaurant in London's Kensington before deciding to go it alone. 'Some of the reviews [at Clarkes] were of dishes I had made and I suddenly realised my own ability. I'd been very insecure up to that point. But this was not me using recipes, this was me deciding. I really started to develop my own style of cooking and it was modern British, very similar to what I'm still doing today, simple with a strong play on seasonality but also a good understanding of Asian philosophies.'

'Black Monday', the 1987 collapse of the British stock market, put paid to Kapoor's clever but ambitious plans. A new career in food writing beckoned when she was invited to review for the Egon Ronay restaurant guide.

Its editor, Drew Smith ('an eccentric genius') was also the editor of the fledgling *Taste* magazine and he offered her a contract. 'I said to him, "I've never written, are you sure you know what you're doing?". He said, "No, but I know your food and if you can't write we'll just use your recipes. No harm done." '

Kapoor's description of *Taste* as 'a tiny team, run on a shoestring' certainly strikes a chord with me, as it will with many magazine editors, but congratulations to Mr Smith, on his bravery and forward thinking. *Taste* only lasted a few years but it is remembered with respect and affection by many British food writers and photographers, it blazed a brilliant trail for *Food Illustrated*, and it discovered Sybil Kapoor. 'I always wanted to write and I just loved it, I took to it like a duck to water', she laughs. 'I also started writing for the *Saturday Telegraph* and then I was offered my first book. The world seemed like my oyster.'

Modern British Food (Penguin, 1995) was followed by *Simply British* (Michael Joseph, 1998). The definition of contemporary British food is a central theme in Kapoor's writing. Her 'mod Brit' recipes in that first issue of *Food Illustrated* might surprise the purist. In addition to the aforementioned profiteroles with their nibbed almonds and kirsch-flavoured cream, there was spring chicken with morels ('particularly good with pappardelle or tagliatelle', wrote Kapoor), roast lamb with mint and wild garlic, burnt lemon cream and a salad of prawns, new potato and rocket. The first book attempted to define British food by seasons, whilst the second is divided into the ingredients that Kapoor considers quintessentially British. Whilst elderflowers, lavender, pheasant and venison don't resonate with my own memories of growing up in England, there is plenty that does: kippers, lamb, shrimp and the detested gooseberries, rhubarb and beetroot of my childhood.

'Aren't we such hopeless cooks that we are forced to plunder from abroad?' wrote Kapoor cheekily in 1998. She believes the British are contradictory when it comes to food. On the one hand, they are experimental and open-minded, happily adopting new flavours as their own (just think of the bizarre cult of chicken tikka masala), whilst clinging to a narrow, almost prejudiced view of what constitutes their national cuisine. 'I would say that British food is anything that is produced or cooked by somebody who lives in Britain. The only way you can perhaps define it more closely is by ingredients. British food is not like French food, which has such fixed rules. We're totally fluid and that's the brilliant thing.'

Pared back is a characteristic that Kapoor considers very British. Her recipes, though actually very varied, carry a trademark delicacy and simplicity. The balance of flavours is paramount and indeed, Kapoor's third book *Taste* (Mitchell Beazley, 2003) explored this. 'I want my food to be exciting and pleasurable but I can't be bothered with very complicated things.' She considers citrus, chilli, soy and ginger to be her signature combination of flavours. 'They're the ones I'm always playing around with, I love their zing.'

The scholar cook has plenty of ideas for the future. A book on our personal relationship with food is of strong interest ('When people come and eat at our table we're giving as strong a message of who we are and what we stand for as what we wear'). But the restaurant that was left on the drawing board back in 1987 is not an option. 'I think the restaurant lifestyle is for when you're younger. I really have a perfect life these days. I've got creativity which I love, I've got writing which I love, I've got my own space and freedom, so to me it's just idyllic.'

'I can still remember the first Chinese meal I ate. It was at Mr Chow's in Knightsbridge, London. I was about eleven years old and thought it was the height of sophistication in Swinging London. Since then, I have tried to incorporate many of its ideas into my cooking. This recipe is typical of my attempts in the late 1990s.'

honey and chilli prawns in lettuce leaves

450 g (1 lb) raw prawn meat (about 750 g/1 lb 10 oz whole raw prawns)
1 small egg white
1 tablespoon cornflour (cornstarch)
2 cloves garlic, crushed
2 tablespoons honey
2 tablespoons white wine vinegar
2 tablespoons soy sauce
4 tablespoons sunflower oil
100 g (3¹/₂ oz/²/₃ cup) salted cashews
¹/₂ teaspoon dried chilli flakes
1 bunch spring onions (scallions), cut into chunks
230 g (8 oz) tin water chestnuts, drained and halved
8 cup-shaped iceberg lettuce leaves

Peel the prawns then lightly score the length of their backs with a sharp knife and remove the dark thread. Rinse and pat dry. Beat the egg white with the cornflour. Mix in the prawns with half the garlic. Cover and chill.

Mix together the honey, vinegar and soy sauce. Set aside.

When ready to eat, heat a large non-stick frying pan or wok over a high heat. Add 3 tablepsoons of the oil and heat until smoking. Add the prawns and cook for 2 minutes, or until coloured on both sides. Remove the prawns from the pan with a slotted spoon and set aside in a bowl.

Take the pan off the heat, quickly add the cashews and chilli flakes and briefly stir-fry until they colour. Add the spicy cashew nuts to the prawns. Return the pan to a high heat, and add the remaining 1 tablespoon oil. Add the remaining garlic, the spring onions and water chestnuts. Stir-fry for 1 minute then return the nuts and prawns to the pan, along with the honey-soy mix. Bring to the boil, let it thicken a little, then spoon into the lettuce leaves and serve.

Serves 4

sybil kapoor

'For me, cooking is all about understanding my ingredients and bringing out their best flavour. This starter epitomizes my desire to pare down recipes to create pure exciting dishes to eat. It comes from my last book Taste: A New Way to Cook. *The simple combination of sourness, bitterness and saltiness brings out the sweetness of the chicory and smoked salmon in a wonderful way.'*

chicory, caper and smoked salmon salad

6 witlof (chicory/Belgian endive), trimmed
2 small red onions, finely sliced
2 heaped tablespoons capers
200 ml (7 fl oz) crème fraîche
2 tablespoons good extra virgin olive oil
2 teaspoons lemon juice
salt and freshly ground black pepper
400g (14 oz/12 slices) finely sliced smoked salmon
1¹/₂ lemons, cut into 12 wedges

Cut the witlof leaves into lengthways strips. Put in a large bowl with the onion. Rinse the capers and pat dry on kitchen paper. Whisk the crème fraîche in a small bowl with 2 tablespoons cold water.

When ready to serve, drizzle the witlof with the olive oil and lemon juice. Toss well, then lightly season with salt and pepper. Divide between 6 plates, then weave in the smoked salmon slices. Scatter with capers, then lightly drizzle the crème fraiche over the salmon. Put the lemon wedges on the side of the plate and serve immediately.

Serves 6

sybil kapoor

'I love chips and will find any excuse to eat them! Not soggy fat chips, but crisp, thin, sea-salted chips. So here are some lightly spiced, lemony veal burgers to accompany my chips. I only ever use organic or ethically reared veal.'

veal burgers with grilled red onions and chips

burgers
2 tablespoons olive oil
1 onion, finely diced
1 red chilli (or to taste),
finely chopped
finely grated zest of 2 lemons
4 tablespoons finely chopped
flat-leaf (Italian) parsley
1/2 tablespoon finely chopped
lemon thyme
500 g (1 lb 2 oz) lean minced veal
salt and freshly ground black pepper

chips
4 large baking potatoes, such as
king edwards
corn oil, for deep-frying
fine sea salt

2 small red onions, sliced
into rounds
3 tablespoons olive oil
crisp green salad, to serve

For the burgers, heat the olive oil in a small frying pan and fry the onion and chilli until soft. Tip into a bowl and mix in the lemon zest, chopped herbs, minced veal, salt and freshly ground black pepper. In the same pan, fry a small patty of the meat mixture and taste to test the seasoning. When you are happy, shape the mix into four burgers. Cover and chill.

For the chips, peel the potatoes and cut into thin chips. Place in a bowl of cold water and leave to soak for 20 minutes to remove excess starch.

Preheat the corn oil in a deep-fryer to 160° C (315° F). Drain the potatoes and spin half in a salad spinner to get rid of excess water, then tip on to kitchen paper and pat dry. Lower into the hot oil and while they cook, repeat the drying process with the second batch. Fry the chips until they have a crisp, uncoloured skin with a soft centre (about 4 minutes). Shake off excess oil before spreading them out to cool on kitchen paper. Repeat with the remaining chips. Once cold, you can chill them until needed.

To serve, preheat the oil again to 180° C (350° F) and cook the chips in batches for about 5 minutes until golden and crisp. Drain on kitchen paper, sprinkle with salt and serve with the veal burgers.

If possible, cook the onion rings and burgers on a barbecue; otherwise, shortly before you are ready to serve, preheat a ribbed, cast-iron grill pan over a medium–high heat. Gently coat the onion rings in 2 tablespoons of the olive oil. Lightly season with salt and pepper. Place on the barbecue or grill pan and cook for about 2 minutes on each side, or until flecked golden and lightly cooked. Remove to a bowl and cover.

Lightly coat the veal burgers with the remaining 1 tablespoon of olive oil and place on the barbecue or grill pan. Cook for about 5 minutes on each side for medium-rare. Serve with the onion rings, chips and a crisp green salad.

Serves 4

123

'Part of the romance of cooking for me has been to try to capture a sense of the seasons and the countryside in my food. One of the ways I try and do this is by infusing dishes with floral scents, such as lavender, elderflower or rose. I created this ice cream in 1997 and it has remained a summer favourite ever since. It is vital that you use unsprayed lavender flowers. The best source is home-grown lavender. If you can't find any Poire Williams, you can use Calvados instead.'

lavender pear ice cream

285 ml (9³/₄ fl oz) thick (double/heavy) cream
2 sprigs lavender flowers
juice of 1 lemon
3 ripe pears, such as Taylor's Gold
4 large egg yolks
170 g (6 oz) caster (superfine) sugar
1 tablespoon Poire Williams liqueur

Place the cream and lavender in a saucepan over low heat. Slowly bring up to scalding point then remove from the heat and leave to infuse for 30 minutes.

Pour the lemon juice into a non-corrosive saucepan. Peel, quarter, core and roughly chop one pear at a time. Thoroughly coat in the lemon juice, to prevent the pear discolouring, before continuing with the remaining fruit. Place over a moderate heat and simmer gently for 10 minutes, or until the fruit is tender. Purée and set aside.

Whisk the egg yolks with the sugar until thick and creamy. Gradually pour in the lavender cream then return to a low heat, stirring continuously with a wooden spoon until it forms a thick custard. This will take around 20 minutes; after the first 5 minutes, remove the lavender. You must not stop stirring or leave the custard unattended during this stage, as it can easily split. Remove from the heat and continue to stir as you add the pear purée followed by the Poire Williams. As soon as the mixture is cool, cover and chill.

Churn the cold custard in an ice-cream machine according to the manufacturer's instructions until it reaches a soft set. This ice cream is particularly good eaten with fresh sugared raspberries.

Serves 6

sybil kapoor

What's the real measure of an Aussie icon? Donna Hay's cookbooks might be on every Australian kitchen shelf (or so it sometimes seems) and her eponymous magazine on smart coffee tables across the land. She might even have been wooed by American lifestyle diva Martha Stewart and have her own homeware range in the department store David Jones, but when Kath Day-Knight announced, in an episode of the ABC's cult comedy *Kath & Kim*, that she was cooking Kel, the hubby-from-hell, 'a Donna Hay', I knew Hay really was a modern food phenomenon.

donna hay

Rewind to 1998 and a phone call to photographer Petrina Tinslay at her Sydney studio about an idea for a Christmas feature in *Food Illustrated*. We wanted an alternative Christmas, perhaps a sun-soaked barbie, as an option to the traditional turkey and trimmings that would, of course, also be in the issue. Tinslay recommended a young food talent called Donna Hay, who at the time was food editor of Australian *marie claire*. The volley of emails that subsequently followed resulted in Donna's intriguingly exotic (at least for a British audience) Christmas menu of oysters with wasabi, Western Australian marrons, Tokay-drenched ice-cream pudding and chocolate and peach panforte wrapped in banana flowers. Absurdly inappropriate for a British Christmas and probably bad editing on my part, but the shots of Donna and friends, picnicking against a backdrop of sparkling water and cloudless skies, more than justified the indulgence — to my mind at least. We published the feature under the heading 'Bay Watch Barbie', which felt quite inspired at the time. There wasn't a barbecue in sight, but that hardly mattered. It was Australia, wasn't it? There must have been one somewhere.

From that feature on, Donna Hay has figured prominently in my working life as a potent mix of friend, muse, adversary and just occasionally, *bête noire*. On her visits to London, we would meet over lunch or dinner and compare notes about our respective magazines. The distinctive signature of white-on-white styling that Donna and Petrina Tinslay perfected (they were a dynamic and almost inseparable team) embodied the cultish, in-demand Australian look. I felt privileged to be invited by her British publisher to launch her first book at Terence Conran's Bluebird Café in Chelsea, where I made a hesitant little speech that suggested the author might have some talent.

In the years that followed, I found myself as Hay's editor in Australia, briefly, at the now-defunct *marie claire Lifestyle*, writing about her frequently for British newspapers and magazines (she once cheekily remarked that I must be making a nice living out of her) and most recently competing with her very successful magazine for its readers and advertising dollars. On a professional level we were daggers, or at least Sabatier knives, drawn (Cherry Ripe, writing in *The Australian* about the launch of *ABC delicious.* and *Donna Hay* magazines in 2001, wanted us to pose with kitchen knives, presumably aimed at each other's throats or backs — we declined) but off the record, I have immense admiration for Donna Hay's clarity of vision, determination and professionalism.

While dissenters might sometimes mutter 'all style, no substance' under their breath ('yes, we love that one', says Hay knowingly), she is nevertheless a huge force for change on the Australian and international food scene. Her five-ingredient recipes and simple food artistry have been, in their way, as motivating and influential as Jamie's cute lisp and cheery chatter.

Still only in her mid-30s, Donna Hay is an international ambassador of Australian food whose meticulous brand of studied minimalism ('simple into special' goes the Hay mantra) has launched a thousand imitators. Her global book sales are stratospheric and her magazine (she left the *marie claire* titles in 2000) outsells traditional rivals such as *Vogue Entertaining + Travel* and *Australian Gourmet Traveller*. Yet over lunch in an inner-Sydney café, Donna Hay is a diffident icon. Conscious of Australia's favourite sport of dead-heading its 'tall poppies' and still smarting from a recent tongue-lashing in an Australian broadsheet, she is more measured and restrained than you'd expect a phenomenon to be. 'I don't want to be on the cutting edge. That's not really me. I'm more about producing stuff of a standard that's always beautiful. My work just evolves, it sort of just happens.'

Hay has always made it clear that her skill and sensitivity for food were not inherited from her own mother. 'My mother still tries to convince me that I inherited my cooking talents from her', she wrote in *Food Illustrated* back in 1998. 'I'm not so sure.' Ask her who her mentors have been and she is similarly reluctant. 'I feel like an upstart when I say I don't have mentors,' she laughs, 'but I have my own vision. I really respect lots of people, but I have a single vision.' Further probing elicits fellow Australians David Thompson and Martin Boetz as chefs she admires (both are masters of Thai cooking, and an Asian aesthetic, in terms of flavour and presentation, is evident in much of Hay's work), but real emotion is reserved for the woman that some see as her role model, others as her alter ego, the American Martha Stewart. 'She's it as far as I'm concerned, I'm still a hardcore fan. I've never met another person whose aura changes the whole feel of the room before she even says a word. She has absolute presence.'

When *Donna Hay Magazine* was launched in 2001, comparisons with *Martha Stewart Living* were inevitable. The two women met when Hay was invited to guest on Stewart's cable television show and Stewart's subsequent offer of a food editing position on her magazine (which Hay declined) is hardly a publishing secret. But Hay has always been quick to deny that she sees herself as an Australian Martha, more so since Stewart's well-documented 2004 misfortunes. 'I don't like being compared to Martha; I could never have that much drive. People don't get it that I don't want to be on the cover of my own magazine but that's not why I started the magazine, to be like Martha.'

I can't help contrasting the ambitious young food stylist I first met in London, styling recipes in a kitchen in the tough, east-end suburb of Hackney (and fretting at its distance from Chelsea), with the steely, self-aware businesswoman in front of me. 'I'm sure that every man at News Corp [her Australian publishers] would say I'm difficult,' she says, as if reading my mind. 'But I see myself very differently to how other people see me, the driven, gung-ho Donna Hay. People think that if I see another stylist with a plate I fancy, I'll run them down and catch the plate before it even hits the ground. I like perfection but at the same time I'm not that driven. I'm Australian, laid-back, whatever will be will be.'

Laid-back? Not driven? The boys at News Corp might be surprised to hear that. This is a woman who once scrubbed out an entire shearing shed on her hands and knees in readiness for a photographic shoot, and served spit-roasted venison and little fig pavlovas to the bewildered shearers. 'Noice', as Kath Day-Knight might say.

'The simple, fresh flavours in this pasta dish make it a success again and again. It genuinely is an office favourite and we still eat it regularly at our staff lunches in the studio, hence its name.'

studio pasta

400 g (14 oz) spaghetti
1¹/₂ tablespoons olive oil
4 long red chillies, seeded and sliced
40 g (1¹/₂ oz/¹/₃ cup) salted capers, rinsed
45 g (1¹/₂ oz/¹/₄ cup) finely grated lemon zest
3 cloves garlic, sliced
150 g (5¹/₂ oz) rocket (arugula), chopped
80 ml (2¹/₂ fl oz/¹/₃ cup) lemon juice
sea salt

Cook the pasta in a large saucepan of salted, boiling water until *al dente*. Drain and return to the saucepan to keep warm. Heat the oil in a frying pan over medium-high heat. Cook the chilli and capers until crisp, then add the lemon zest and garlic and cook for a further 1–2 minutes, or until golden. Toss with the pasta, rocket, lemon juice and salt and serve immediately.

Serves 6

'I usually don't re-run recipes but this one caused such a stir in the launch issue of marie claire *that I decided it merited a place in my first book.*

I love this recipe and clearly so did the readers of the book. When I travelled on an author tour a year after it was published, I met so many people who had cooked it and they were all raving about it. It was so strange to think that people from Sydney to London and Vancouver to New York had all enjoyed the exact same dish.'

grilled balsamic chicken with limes

3 tablespoons balsamic vinegar,
plus extra for sprinkling
2 cloves garlic, crushed
2 tablespoons olive oil
cracked black pepper
4 skinless, boneless chicken breasts
4 limes, halved
assorted salad greens

Combine the vinegar, garlic, oil and pepper and pour over the chicken. Allow the chicken to marinate for 5 minutes, then remove from the marinade.

Cook the fillets on a preheated barbecue or chargrill for 1–2 minutes on each side, or until cooked through. While the chicken is cooking, place the limes on the barbecue or grill to caramelize.

To serve, arrange the salad greens on serving plates. Slice the chicken and place on top of the greens. Sprinkle with extra balsamic vinegar and serve with the limes.

Serves 4

'This isn't technically a recipe, but it's still one of my favourites when it comes to showing our readers something that's so simple but with a twist. Who would have thought that dribbling flavoured topping down tall glasses would cause such a stir? But people still talk about it! Whether it's for a child or just a child at heart, it keeps them busy for ages.'

striped milkshakes

strawberry or lime topping
milk
vanilla ice cream

Spoon stripes of topping down the inside of each glass. Carefully pour in milk until three-quarters full and top with a scoop of ice cream. Serve with straws.

'Two of my favourite things crushed together — vanilla ice cream and raspberries — yum. This recipe is so easy but always causes a stir when I serve it as an afternoon treat or for dessert. Only one downside — never any leftovers.'

crushed raspberry semifreddo

3 eggs
2 egg yolks, extra
1/2 teaspoon vanilla extract
230 g (8 oz/1 cup) caster (superfine) sugar
500 g (1 lb 2 oz) frozen raspberries
435 ml (15 1/4 fl oz/1 3/4 cups) whipping cream

Line the base of an 8 x 26 cm (3 1/4 x 10 1/2 inch) loaf tin with baking (parchment) paper.

Place the eggs, extra yolks, vanilla and sugar in a heatproof bowl. Place over a saucepan of simmering water and whisk the mixture for 4–5 minutes, or until heated through and frothy. Remove from the heat and beat with an electric mixer until pale and thick. Lightly crush or break up 300 g (10 1/2 oz) of the raspberries and gently fold through the egg mixture. Set aside.

Beat the cream in the bowl of an electric mixer until very soft peaks form. Gently fold the egg mixture into the cream until just combined. Arrange the remaining raspberries in the base of the prepared tin and pour over the semifreddo mixture. Cover with foil and freeze for 24 hours, or until firm. To serve, remove from the tin and cut into thick slices.

Serves 6–8

peter gordon

The Sugar Club restaurant was quite a phenomenon in London in the mid-90s. Its location on the 'wrong' side of Notting Hill added a frisson of danger that no doubt appealed to the clientele. Madonna ate there, which shouldn't have mattered a bit, but of course it did. Fay Maschler, the influential *London Evening Standard* restaurant critic, lauded it. And the Sugar Club had Peter Gordon, the sexy Kiwi chef with the buccaneer earring, who flouted the rules with his controversial 'fusion' cooking.

When I first met Peter Gordon in 1997, The Sugar Club had been open for less than two years. *Time Out* magazine had already voted it Best Modern British Restaurant in its annual awards (while, confusingly, the *London Evening Standard* named it Best Pacific Rim restaurant), his *Sugar Club Cookbook* had hit the shelves and he was one of the most talked-about young chefs in London, dividing opinions as fast as he could combine flavours. He was riding the wave of a style of cooking that clashed cultures and flavours in a way that — in Britain at least — sometimes felt like culinary heresy. Among Gordon's dishes on the original Sugar Club menu were an entrée of black cardamom-braised pig's cheek on soba noodles and puy lentils. There was roast guinea fowl on wok-fried Spanish black beans with bok choy and tomato chilli jam or a yoghurt bavarois served with poached tamarillo and a brandy snap. Fusion's alternative tag, Pacific Rim, acknowledged that its roots lay in the more stylistically *laissez faire* kitchens of Gordon's native New Zealand and of Australia, where he had served his apprenticeship. Fusion cooking suddenly proliferated in London, although rarely with Gordon's finesse. Instinct told me his would be a timely and unusual voice in *Food Illustrated* and as luck would have it, he could write.

His back-page column ran in the first nine issues of the magazine and in it he wrote simply and lyrically of his memories of a New Zealand childhood, the travels in South-east Asia that so influenced him and his fascination for unusual flavours. He even entered the debate over his own cooking. 'It's a shame that critics are so divided', Gordon wrote in May 1998, 'and sad that some arrive at the table armed with prejudices. No matter how brilliant and respected classical cuisine might be, cooking is a living art which changes and develops as do the people who are eating and preparing it. Enjoy it. Fusion food tastes good.'

Gordon, who had also been the chef of the original Sugar Club restaurant in Wellington, New Zealand, in the mid-80s, was bemused by the furore his cooking created. Talking over lunch late in 2004 at his current London restaurant The Providores (Gordon is also consultant chef to the acclaimed Public in New York, and to Changa, a restaurant in Istanbul, Turkey), and despite the fact that London has had almost a decade to get used to his way of doing things, he still sounds defensive. 'I think they [his London contemporaries] have a fear of what I do because they don't understand it. They're trained in one school of thought, whether it be southern French or northern Italian, and I think a lot of them would say fusion food is ridiculous.'

But his cooking was never any random collision of ingredients and ethnicities. To Gordon, the balance of 'acidity, density, sweetness and texture' is everything, and fortunately for The Sugar Club (which relocated to London's Soho in 1998) he was — and still is — a master of that balance. In another of his *Food Illustrated* columns, in October 1998, Gordon revealed his subtle understanding of flavour. 'In a remote Malaysian village I ate baby squid cooked in a sugar syrup and stuffed with sticky rice. While it wasn't awful, it just seemed too strange until someone sprinkled some dried chilli flakes on top and then the dish came to life, the flavours gelling at last.'

Gordon clearly remembers his food epiphany. 'It was at Kuni's, a Japanese restaurant in Melbourne. I had the silken tofu with shaved bonito and daikon and it was just the most amazing thing I'd ever had.' At the time (the early 80s) he was studying at Melbourne's respected William Angliss catering college. 'I said to the tutor, "Why are we not doing any of this?" and he said, "The Japanese don't even cook, they eat everything raw. This is a serious college." '

When he tells a story like that, it's easy to understand the anarchy. That's a strong word but in the food world, Gordon is something of an anarchist. Jill Norman, the respected food writer and editor, has described Gordon very aptly as having 'no allegiance to anything but a great understanding of everything'. Running my eye over the menu at The Providores, there's less insistence on Asian flavours than in his Sugar Club days, but the dishes can still sound alarmingly complex in their construction. There's an entrée of roast foie gras on a toasted ajowan crumpet (ajowan is a spice similar to cumin) with Russian cress and chillied pineapple compote. Then New Zealand venison loin on polenta and bok choy with a pomegranate *nam pla* dressing. Gordon's food is not, admittedly, for the faint-hearted. 'The world is full of ingredients and wherever we're from, whether or not it's part of our native cuisine,' he explains, 'it doesn't mean we can't use them if we're not from that region. Italians are horrified when I throw lemon grass in a risotto, but lemon grass and rice are Asian and parmesan cheese certainly isn't! My philosophy with a new ingredient is always "What can I do with it?". I never think "Well, it's a Thai ingredient, so it has to be a Thai dish".'

Gordon has lived in London since 1989 but still considers New Zealand to be his spiritual home. He visits as often as he can. 'That feeling I get as the plane flies into Auckland is something I get nowhere else in the world.' His links with New Zealand are strong. A restaurant consultancy in Auckland takes him there at least four times a year, in addition to which there's the consultancy to Air New Zealand (Gordon's food is served on flights between London and Los Angeles) and his long-standing monthly contributions to New Zealand *House & Garden* magazine. For a time he was even the face of New Zealand Lamb, so to speak. But London has been home for more than fifteen years. 'I love London, I love being so close to Europe. London is such a mixed bag, you feel like you're in a Benetton ad wherever you go. What I don't like about

London is the stuff that's beyond my control. There's eight million people here, it's bound to be messy and dirty and congested but that's also its appeal.'

Gordon has dabbled with television over the years. There were appearances on both Nigel Slater's and Jamie Oliver's series and a thirteen-part series for a British food network that he would rather forget ('I think it was made on a budget of about one pound fifty. I started the passionfruit parfait in a green shirt and finished it in a red one.') He admits he's something of a purist when it comes to television and he knows the budgets just don't exist for the sort of projects he'd like to do.

But when would he find time for television anyway? There are already enough plates spinning in the Gordon universe. There's the charity work, raising funds for leukaemia research, for the Children's Fire and Burns Trust (Gordon was scalded himself as a child) and his support for the Link Foundation, which promotes educational exchanges between New Zealand and Britain. Then there's The Providores, the overseas consultancies, the new project in Auckland, the magazine columns, the demos. He's excited by the growing interest in his food in the United States (the success of Public has ensured that) and would like to do more in Australia. 'Australia is probably the foodie country of the universe and it's where I trained and got all my inspiration.'

I hope we see more of him in Australia, too. He's passionate and honest and cooks brave, complex, thought-provoking food. And he's been in Britain all those years but still says 'brekkie'. He's got to be all right.

'Try your best to get hold of fresh silken tofu for this, although the tetra-packed stuff will be okay. In summer, make the corn purée from fresh sweetcorn. In winter, canned or frozen corn will do.'

ramen noodles with creamed sesame sweetcorn, crisp tofu and toasted walnuts

500 g (1 lb 2 oz) tofu, cut into
2.5 cm (1 inch) cubes
350 g (12 oz/1³/₄ cups) sweetcorn
kernels
250 ml (9 fl oz/1 cup) pouring cream
2 spring onions (scallions), sliced
2 teaspoons sesame seeds, toasted
90 g (3¹/₄ oz/¹/₂ cup) finely ground
rice flour
1 teaspoon salt
1/2 teaspoon *pimenton dulce* (sweet
smoked Spanish paprika)
50 ml (1¹/₂ fl oz) peanut oil
60 g (2¹/₄ oz/¹/₂ cup) walnut pieces,
roughly chopped
200 g (7 oz) ramen noodles, boiled
until cooked, then drained and
tossed in a little peanut oil
12 chives, finely sliced

Place the tofu cubes on uncoloured paper towels for 30 minutes to extract some of the water.

Meanwhile, put the corn, cream, spring onion and sesame seeds in a small pan, bring to the boil and simmer, uncovered, until the cream has reduced by half. Purée in a blender or small food processor, check the seasoning and keep warm.

Combine the flour, salt and paprika and use this to coat the tofu. Heat half the oil in a frying pan to moderate heat and cook half the tofu until golden on all sides. Remove to a warm plate and cook the remaining tofu. Add the remaining oil and gently fry the walnuts until just golden.

To serve, place a quarter of the corn cream on to each plate, place a pile of noodles on top and then some tofu. Scatter with the walnuts and sprinkle with chives.

Serves 4 as a starter

peter gordon

'This rather time-consuming recipe is well worth the effort. Get it smoking on the barbecue and it'll seem less of a trial. The broth also makes a great soup, especially when bulked out with noodles, crab claws and crisp shallots.'

curry-leaf-crusted snapper on roast sweet potato with smoked coconut tamarind broth and plantain chips

$^1/_2$ cup fresh curry leaves
two 500 g (1 lb 2 oz) snapper, filleted, scales and pin bones removed (reserve all the bones)
$^1/_2$ cup untreated wood chips (or tea leaves)
50 g (1$^3/_4$ oz/$^1/_4$ cup) rice
2 red chillies (1 whole, the other split, deseeded and julienned)
2 cloves garlic
50 g (1$^3/_4$ oz) ginger
2 stems lemon grass
6 lime leaves
oil, for frying
1 red onion, peeled and sliced
80 g (2$^3/_4$ oz) block tamarind, seeds and all
400 ml (14 fl oz) unsweetened coconut milk
about 1$^1/_2$ tablespoons Thai fish sauce
50 ml (1$^1/_2$ fl oz) lime juice
1 large orange sweet potato, unpeeled
1 green plantain
sea salt, to taste
light olive oil, for drizzling
2 spring onions (scallions), thinly sliced, to serve
$^1/_2$ bunch coriander (cilantro), leaves picked off and stem cut into 1 cm ($^1/_2$ inch) pieces

Scatter half the curry leaves on a sheet of plastic wrap. Lay the snapper fillets on top, season well and scatter over the remaining curry leaves. Wrap tightly and leave to rest in a cool place until ready.

Line a wok with foil and sprinkle in the wood chips and rice. Place a cake rack in the wok and sit the reserved fish bones on it, turn the heat up, put a tight-fitting lid on and smoke for 10 minutes.

In a food processor, blitz the whole chilli, garlic, ginger, lemon grass and lime leaves. Heat up a pan, add a little oil and fry the onion until caramelized. Add the blitzed aromatics and fry until smelling sweet, then add the smoked bones and break it all up with a spoon. Add the tamarind and coconut milk and 100 ml (3$^1/_2$ fl oz) water. Bring to a boil, then reduce heat and simmer for 15 minutes. Strain through a fine sieve then season with fish sauce and lime juice. Keep warm.

Meanwhile, steam or boil the sweet potato until almost cooked then place under cold running water to cool. Slice into rings about 3 cm (1$^1/_4$ inches) thick, place on a baking tray lined with baking paper and roast at 200° C (400° F/Gas 6) until done. Peel the plantain and finely slice it on a mandolin. Deep-fry in small batches at 140° C (275° F) until crisp, then drain well and sprinkle with sea salt.

When ready to serve, unwrap the fish and drizzle with a little oil. Heat a non-stick pan with a lid and when fiercely hot add the fish, skin side down, and put the lid back on. Cook for 1–2 minutes depending on the thickness of the fillets, then turn the fish over and take the pan off the heat, keeping the lid on. So the leaves don't burn, keep an eye on them and keep the lid on the whole time.

Divide the sweet potato among 4 pasta bowls. Place a piece of fish on top of each, ladle the broth over, then scatter with the julienned chilli, plantain, spring onion and coriander.

Serves 4 as a main course

Opposite: curry-leaf-crusted snapper on roast sweet potato with smoked coconut tamarind broth and plantain chips
Above: pork belly hot-pot with chilli, baby beetroot, morels and miso

'I bought the pork belly for this recipe already roasted from Chinatown because I was lazy — you can cook it yourself, but that's another recipe. This dish can be made in the morning and thrown in the oven an hour before you want to eat it, so it's great for dinner parties, either made as one huge bowl or as individual ones. Various types of miso paste are available from Japanese and health-food stores, and some Asian stores. The paler it is, the more subtle — so perhaps start with shiro *(white) miso.'*

pork belly hot-pot with chilli, baby beetroot, morels and miso

800 g (1 lb 12 oz) boneless roasted pork belly
16 dried morels
2 knobs fresh ginger, peeled and thinly sliced
6 cloves garlic, peeled and sliced
1–2 red chillies, sliced into rings
2 black cardamom pods
16 small beetroot (beets), boiled or roasted until cooked, then peeled
1½ heaped tablespoons miso paste
250 ml (9 fl oz/1 cup) dry sherry
2 tablespoons light soy sauce

Preheat the oven to 200° C (400° F/Gas 6). Cut the pork belly into 2 cm (³/₄ inch) cubes.

Soak the morels in 400 ml (14 fl oz) for 15 minutes.

Take morels from the soaking water (reserve the water) and rinse gently to remove any grit. Place in a ceramic dish with a tight-fitting lid. Add the ginger, garlic, chilli, cardamom and beetroot, then scatter the pork over.

Whisk the miso into the sherry, soy and the strained mushroom water then pour this over the pork. Cover the dish tightly, place in the oven and cook for 1 hour. It should now be heated through and bubbling — if not, cook for 20–30 minutes more. Serve with steamed rice or plain noodles.

Serves 4 as a main course

peter gordon

'This dessert has a good contrast in texture and flavour. The tamarillos will taste quite sour no matter how ripe they are, but this works well with the cake, which is quite rich and dense. The cake is a wonderful dairy- and wheat-free invention, with no eggs, and if the chocolate you use has no dairy products in it, then the cake is vegan too — if you skip the whipped cream!'

oven-baked tamarillos with whipped cream and chocolate tofu and den miso cake

4 tamarillos
80 g (2³/₄ oz/¹/₃ cup) caster (superfine) sugar
80 g (2³/₄ oz) dark chocolate
80 g (2³/₄ oz) milk chocolate
160 g (5¹/₂ oz) firm tofu
1 stem-ginger ball
100 g (3¹/₂ oz) *den miso* (*shiro miso* cooked with sake, mirin and sugar)
150 ml (5 fl oz) whipping cream (optional, but makes the dessert very delicious)

Line a 15 cm (6 inch) square cake tin with baking (parchment) paper.

Preheat the oven to 160° C (315° F/Gas 2–3). Cut the tamarillos in half lengthways and lay them, cut side up, on a baking tray lined with baking (parchment) paper. Sprinkle with the sugar and bake until shrivelled a little, but still juicy, just like an oven-roasted tomato — about 90 minutes.

Turn the oven up to 180° C (350° F/Gas 4).

Melt the chocolate in bowl covered in plastic wrap over simmering water. Place the tofu, stem ginger and *den miso* in a food processor and blend. Whisk in the chocolate and then pour the mixture into the prepared tin and bake for 16 minutes. Remove from the oven, cool then place in the fridge.

To serve, remove the cake from the fridge and invert onto a board then cut into whichever shape you want. Lightly whip the cream. Place two tamarillo halves on the plate with a piece of the cake and a dollop of the cream.

Serves 4

145

In the June 1998 issue of *Food Illustrated*, we ran a feature entitled 'The Last Jews of Cochin'. Beautifully photographed by our 'man in India', Jason Lowe (he was actually based in London but seemed to spend most of his time on the subcontinent), it was a fascinating study of the food traditions of the dwindling Jewish community of Cochin, in southern India, and in particular, the cooking of Queenie Hallegua, an Indian woman of Jewish descent. This feature has always represented to me what the magazine stood for, to surprise the reader with intriguing and unusual stories that they were unlikely to have read or seen elsewhere.

claudia roden

The feature was evocatively written by Claudia Roden, the respected London-based food writer generally regarded as the foremost authority on Middle Eastern and Jewish food. Quietly but precisely spoken, with a strong accent despite her many years in Britain, the Egyptian-born writer and I first met over lunch in 1998 at Giorgio Locatelli's Zafferano restaurant in London. Roden had recently published her magnum opus (if a writer can be allowed more than one magnum opus, then Roden has produced several), *The Book of Jewish Food* (Viking, 1997). I cannot remember what we ate on that occasion other than *carta di musica*, the delicious, paper-thin Sardinian bread whose provenance Roden explained so carefully as we ate.

Seven years later, I find myself sampling *bohsalino* in her cosy, bohemian North London kitchen. A Lebanese sweet made from crushed pistachio and rose water, the *bohsalino* is filled — rather alarmingly in my view — with thick clotted cream, and we are debating whether the recipe should be included in her new book, a study of the food of Lebanon, Turkey and Morocco. The conversation turns to *The Book of Jewish Food*, for which Roden won numerous awards and which was sixteen years in the researching and writing. 'The trouble is I do love big subjects,' she laughs, 'but there came a point when my publisher said "You'll never, ever finish because it's endless." In the end she just said "Claudia, it's finished, give it to me!".'

147

Reluctant to describe herself as a food historian, Roden nevertheless approaches her subject with an academic's exhaustive attention to detail, researching old manuscripts and travelling and reading extensively. As most of her books will testify, it is the lineage and ancestry of food that fascinate her. In her seminal *Book of Middle Eastern Food*, for example, published in 1968, Roden linked the food of fourteen countries stretching from Morocco to Iraq, far beyond the bounds of what we normally understand as the Middle East. And in *The Book of Jewish Food*, she silenced the dissenters — who claimed there was no such thing — by tracing the food traditions of the two distinct Jewish cultures, Ashkenazi and Sephardi, across the world. As she writes in her introduction to the book, 'because a culture is complex this does not mean it does not exist'.

Claudia Roden was born in Cairo, Egypt, of Syrian Jewish descent. When the Suez Crisis broke in 1956, her family fled Egypt, and Roden finished her schooling in Paris. She then studied art in London under such luminaries as Anthony Caro and Elizabeth Frink at St Martin's College of Art. But food — and the food of her homeland, in particular — remained a passion (on arriving in Britain, she was delighted to find *melokhia*, a traditional Egyptian soup, in Elizabeth David's *Book of Mediterranean Food*) and even a recurring theme in her art. A canvas on her kitchen wall — one of her own from her student days — is of men eating. 'They're North African workers in a Paris café. I was interested in people eating, even then.'

Roden recalls that in those days, in Britain, food was a taboo subject. 'I would ask the neighbours what they were cooking and they'd look at me with horror. Even if you went to dinner you would never make a remark about the food.

It just wasn't done.' Collecting recipes therefore became a private passion, fuelled by research trips to the British Library, where she studied translations of 12th- and 13th-century Arabic texts.

'Most of the dishes were names that I knew. I had always thought maybe we were eating some funny food that only our family ate, but I could see that we were part of an old tradition.' This was the point at which Roden realized 'a dish is not just a dish, it's not just something to eat, it's got a whole history and it's part of a civilization. It's not from nowhere.'

'I realized that something had to be done', she explains. 'I was never going to be a great painter but I thought that [recording the recipes] would be valuable, and that we might lose them forever if they weren't written down.' The subsequent *Book of Middle Eastern Food* was published in 1968 and has never been out of print since. It was far-sighted of original publisher Thomas Nelson to publish a book of Middle Eastern recipes in the late 60s, but it was no surprise to her that when the book was published, 'nobody took any notice, no reviews, not one'. But as she explains, 'I didn't want to be a professional food writer. I thought I was only going to write this one book and I was brought up in a society where a woman shouldn't earn anything. Even when my book came out, my father was ashamed if anyone asked him about it. He'd say "Oh, she doesn't earn anything from it, it's just for love".'

'But I do think you get addicted to the subject of food.' Roden smiles almost apologetically, as if excusing her subsequent career as one of Britain's most respected — and awarded — food writers. To date she has received five Glenfiddich Awards plus numerous overseas accolades, including a Dutch award for her contribution to Middle Eastern culture. That career has included authoritative books on Mediterranean cooking, coffee, the revised *New Book of Middle Eastern Food* (1985) and, of course, *The Book of Jewish Food*. An acclaimed series of articles written by Roden on regional Italian food for *The Sunday Times Magazine* outraged one London restaurateur, who perhaps felt the commission should have been his ('He said, "Claudia, you should keep to your patch!" '), but the Italians obviously disagreed, awarding her one of their most prestigious food prizes for the series.

Roden's kitchen feels a little like hallowed ground. I remember that it's where I first met Stephanie Alexander and Maggie Beer and I know that the late Elizabeth David, and food writers Richard Olney and Jane Grigson, all dined at this table. Roden, unique amongst most contemporary food writers, met David on many occasions. I ask if she was as difficult as her reputation suggests. Roden answers carefully. 'She was always nice to me, but not that nice. She was distant, but we all respected her enormously.' Roden recalls the time she was going to New York and David asked if she would take a gift to her great friend, the food writer James Beard. 'It was some powder to tenderize meat. It was a dangerous thing to bring white powder into America but it didn't seem to attract any interest.'

Claudia Roden, perhaps in the traditions of her heritage, is a natural storyteller. Her conversation is wonderfully discursive, flowing easily from subject to subject, memory to memory. Occasionally she pauses mid-sentence to find *le mot juste* and I am reminded that English is no more her mother tongue than the French she spoke as a girl in Cairo. We have talked about her children (she has three, and five grandchildren) but not of her marriage. I respect the fact that she would prefer not to. With a smile, however, and as a perfect example of the schism (Roden is Sephardi, her ex-husband was Ashkenazi, of Russian–Jewish descent), even in food, within the Jewish cultures, she recounts that at their wedding, her ex-husband's mother said, 'I will never eat your fancy food, so don't expect me to.' One wonders whether she bought the book instead.

'These dainty little rolls were never absent from our buffet and tea tables. We learnt to make them as children. Use large sheets of filo (sizes vary), cut into strips. If the sheets are too thin, the pastry is liable to tear and the filling can burst out during cooking. In that case, use two strips together, brushing with butter in between; you will then need double the number of sheets. I prefer to use only one strip, as it makes for a lighter pastry. The rolls can be made in advance and reheated.'

little filo cheese rolls

100 g (3½ oz) feta cheese, mashed with a fork
100 g (3½ oz) cottage cheese
1 egg, lightly beaten
3 tablespoons chopped mint or dill, optional
8 large sheets of filo
75 g (2½ oz) butter, melted

For the filling, mix the feta with the cottage cheese, egg and herbs.

Take out the sheets of filo only when you are ready to use them, since they dry out quickly. Cut them into 4 strips measuring about 30 x 12 cm (12 x 4½ inches) and put them in a pile on top of each other. Brush the top strip with melted butter. Take a tablespoon of filling. Place it at one short end of the strip in a thin sausage shape along the edge — about 2 cm (¾ inch) from the end and 2 cm (¾ inch) from the side edges. Roll up the filo with the filling inside, like a cigarette. Fold in the ends about one-third of the way along to trap the filling and then continue to roll.

Do the same with the remaining strips of filo and cheese filling. Place the rolls, seam side down, on a baking tray and brush the tops with the melted butter. Bake at 150° C (300° F/Gas 2) for 30 minutes, or until crisp and golden.

Makes 16

claudia roden

'Many of the dishes popular in the court kitchens of Constantinople in Ottoman times spread throughout the Empire. This pilaf is one of the classics that you find in Cairo and all the cities that were once the outposts of the Empire.'

roasted chicken with pine nut and raisin pilaf

1 large chicken
2 tablespoons extra virgin olive oil
salt and pepper

for the pilaf
400 g (14 oz) long-grain or basmati rice
1 large onion, chopped
3 tablespoons sunflower oil
100 g (3½ oz/⅔ cup) pine nuts
750 ml (26 fl oz/3 cups) hot chicken stock
½ teaspoon ground allspice
1 teaspoon ground cinnamon
salt and pepper
3 tablespoons currants or tiny black raisins
60–75 g (2–2½ oz) butter, cut into small pieces

Preheat the oven to 200° C (400° F/Gas 6).

Rub the chicken with a mixture of olive oil, salt and pepper. Put it, breast side down, in a roasting tin so that the fat runs down; this prevents the breasts from drying out. Add 4 tablespoons of water to the pan. Roast for 1 hour in the preheated oven, then turn the chicken breast side up and continue to cook for 15–30 minutes, depending on the size of the chicken, until it is well done and brown.

While the chicken is cooking, prepare the pilaf. Wash the rice by pouring cold water over it, then stir well and leave to soak for a few minutes. Drain, then rinse with cold running water.

In a large pan, fry the onion in the oil until soft and golden. Add the pine nuts and stir until lightly coloured. Add the rice and stir over a moderate heat until it is well coated with fat. Then add the hot stock and stir in the allspice, cinnamon, salt (you need to take into consideration the saltiness of the stock), pepper and the currants or raisins. Bring to the boil, then simmer, covered and undisturbed, over a low heat for 20 minutes, or until the rice is tender and the water absorbed. Add a little extra water if it looks necessary.

Stir in the butter, check the seasoning and serve hot with the chicken.

Serves 4–6

claudia roden

'This is one of my favourites. It makes a good first course as well as a vegetarian main dish. The vegetables can be served hot or cold and the yoghurt should be at room temperature. I mix the two kinds of yoghurt — full-fat natural yoghurt and the thick "Greek style" — to get a thick, creamy texture that still pours well.'

roasted eggplant and capsicum with yoghurt and pine nuts

4 small eggplants (aubergines),
about 1 kg (2 lb 4 oz) total
3 large red capsicums (peppers)
1 tablespoon lemon juice
4 tablespoons extra virgin olive oil
salt and black pepper
125 g (4^1/$_2$ oz/^{1}/$_2$ cup) full-fat plain
(natural) yoghurt
125 g (4^1/$_2$ oz/^{1}/$_2$ cup) Greek-style
yoghurt, strained
2 cloves garlic, crushed
50 g (1^3/$_4$ oz/^{1}/$_3$ cup) pine nuts

Preheat the oven to to 220° C (425° F/Gas 7).

Prick the eggplants with a pointed knife to prevent them exploding in the oven. Place the eggplants and capsicums on a large piece of foil on a baking tray and roast for 45–60 minutes, or until the eggplants feel soft when you press them. Turn the capsicums one half turn after 25 minutes, and take them out before the eggplants, when they are soft and their skins are blackened in places.

As the capsicums come out of the oven, drop them in a freezer bag and twist to seal it closed. When cool enough to handle, peel them, remove the stems and seeds, and cut them in half or in 4 long strips.

When the eggplants are cool enough to handle, peel them into a colander. Press the flesh gently to let the juices run out. Cut each into 4 pieces and turn them in a little lemon juice to prevent them discolouring.

Put the eggplants and capsicums on one side of a shallow serving plate. Dress with 3 tablespoons olive oil, salt and pepper and mix gently. Mix the two types of yoghurt together, beat in the garlic and some salt, and pour onto the other side of the plate.

Just before serving, fry the pine nuts very briefly in the remaining oil, stirring, until very lightly browned, and sprinkle over the yoghurt.

Serves 6

claudia roden

'This crisp vermicelli-like pastry with a cream filling, which is eaten hot with a fragrant syrup poured over, was an important party dish in our Jewish community in Egypt, as it was in Syria. Moslems made it with a bland white cheese, Jews favoured a cream filling with ground rice. It is very easy to make, but konafa — the pastry also sold under the Greek name kataifi — *is not easy to find. Only a few Oriental stores and the occasional bakery that sells fresh filo sell it.'*

konafa à la creme

for the syrup
500 g (1 lb 2 oz/2¼ cups) sugar
300 ml (10½ fl oz) water
2 tablespoons lemon juice
2 tablespoons orange blossom water

for the filling
125 g (4½ oz) ground rice
950 ml (33 fl oz) milk
125 ml (4 fl oz/½ cup) thick
(double/heavy) cream
4 tablespoons sugar

for the pastry
500 g (1 lb 2 oz) *kataifi*
250 g (9 oz/1 cup) unsalted butter,
melted
100 g (3½ oz/¾ cup) pistachio
nuts, coarsely chopped,
to garnish

Make the syrup first; boil the sugar, water and lemon juice for 5–10 minutes until it is just thick enough to coat a spoon, then add the orange blossom water. Let it cool, then chill in the refrigerator.

Perheat the oven to 180° C (350° F/Gas 4).

For the filling, mix the ground rice with enough cold milk to make a smooth paste. Bring the rest of the milk with the cream to the boil. Add the ground rice paste, stirring vigorously with a wooden spoon so as not to let lumps form. Leave on very low heat and continue to stir constantly until the mixture thickens, being careful not to let it burn at the bottom. Add the sugar and stir well.

Put the *kataifi* in a large bowl and pull the strands apart to loosen them. Pour on the slightly cooled melted butter then work it in with your hands so that the strands are thoroughly coated. Spread half the pastry over the bottom of a large 30 cm (12 inch) round pie dish. Spread the thickened milk mixture over it evenly and cover with the rest of the pastry. Press down and flatten with the palm of your hand. Bake for about 45 minutes. Some like to brown the bottom (which becomes the top when the pastry is turned out) by running it very briefly over heat on a hob. Others prefer the pastry to remain pale.

Just before serving, run a sharp knife round the edges of the pastry to loosen the sides and turn out onto a large serving dish. Pour the cold syrup all over and sprinkle the top with the chopped pistachios. Alternatively, you can pour only half the syrup before serving and pass the rest in a pitcher for everyone to help themselves to more.

Serves 12

'Was it 1998? I'm so terrible with dates. Things have a habit of leaving my psyche', laughs Maggie Beer as we sit chatting at her remote farm shop in South Australia's Barossa Valley. It's a late winter morning but the air is already thrumming with heat. We're sipping 'sour grapes', a pretty rose-tinted drink ('like drinking champagne') that Beer has created from her favourite verjuice. It is unspeakably delicious and I declare it ready to hit the shelves immediately. Ever the perfectionist, Beer shakes her head, commenting that 'the bead still isn't quite as it should be'.

maggie beer

It was indeed 1998 when I first met Maggie Beer — cook, food writer and provedore — who was in the United Kingdom with Stephanie Alexander to promote the Tuscan cookbook they wrote together. The occasion was a magnificent Sunday lunch at the home of fellow writer Claudia Roden, where Stephanie and Maggie cooked and entertained with anecdotes from their Italian adventure. Alexander's was the more familiar name, but I remember being in thrall of Beer's easy warmth, generous spirit and capacity for laughter. In a suburban London kitchen, both women embodied all that seemed exotic and seductive — to a Brit at least — about Australians.

To interview Maggie Beer for this book, it was important to cross Australia to the region that has been her home for more than 30 years and with which her name is synonymous. To meet Beer in Sydney, as I have done several times over the years, is to meet only part of her. I wanted to understand the Barossa and her relationship with it.

To an outsider, and especially to a non-Australian, the verdant Barossa, just a couple of hours from Adelaide, is an unusual find. This is a church-scattered landscape of small villages and settlements, with an extraordinary sense of its own heritage. Many of the occupants of the Barossa are descended from German-speaking Silesians who settled there in the mid-19th century. Take a walk through the town of Hahndorf and count the number of traditional German butchers and bakers with their *mettwurst* and *streuselkuchen*. It's remarkable.

'I've never had such a feeling of community in my life', she explains. 'The Barossa is very physically beautiful and the work ethic of the people here is phenomenal.' Beer, who divides her life in the valley between her home, her farm shop and her export kitchen, is part of the Barossa landscape. She is its best-known spokesperson, rarely missing an opportunity to promote and write about the region and its bounty. Some of Australia's finest food producers are in this abundant little fold of the continent. Yet Beer is not originally from the Barossa; she's what they would call a 'blow-in', moving there from Sydney in the early 1970s with her husband Colin.

'I spent my youth in Sydney's west, which was a cultural desert in those days, but I always had ingenuity and decided to travel.' She went first to New Zealand and then to Europe, where she worked as a nurse and an air stewardess, and ran a bar in Scotland. She had never cooked anything in her life when she landed a job as a cook in a sailing school. 'But I had the gift of the gab and this was the 1960s, when people didn't have to have credentials.' She returned to Australia, met Colin Beer (whose family hail from the Barossa) and married him in 1970. When they moved to the Barossa from Sydney in 1973, Beer was pregnant with her first daughter, Saskia. 'I was just bowled over by the place. You can smell the seasons here, feel their rhythm.'

I sense that the early years in the Barossa were a struggle, Beer working as a land broker to pay the bills while Colin turned his hand to rearing pheasants. Maggie Beer's trilogy of books (*Maggie's Farm*, *Maggie's Orchard* and *Maggie's Table*) document those early years and the celebrated Pheasant Farm Restaurant, which the couple ran until 1993. Though the restaurant doors have long since closed, the pheasant — or an approximation of it — remains the Maggie Beer logo and despite a growing range of products, it is still the pheasant pâté, along with verjuice and quince paste, for which she is known best.

Maggie Beer left school at the age of 14. Early in our conversation she admits that 'not having had an education, I always felt I'd failed.' Perhaps this explains the drive and determination to succeed that even she admits can be challenging to those around her. 'My staff either love me or they don't stay. I'm driven always to do better. I never lose my temper but I'm only interested in working with people who see that continuous improvement is part of life. I'm a Capricorn

and I have their pedantic, anal-retentive nature. Almost pigheaded.' She reflects for a moment on her words. 'Well, almost.'

Beer laughingly admits that she has taken 20 years 'to become an overnight sensation'. Like so many of her peers, she counts Elizabeth David as an inspiration ('what I loved about her was the concept of octopus, aioli and avocado … it was never the recipe but the floating of an idea') along with her great friend Stephanie Alexander, and the American food writers Paula Wolfert and Madeleine Kamman. 'When you love food you can taste something as you read it.'

These days she travels frequently, both as an ambassador for Australian produce and the Barossa in particular, or to visit her overseas markets. 'I love Italy for the heart and Japan for the aesthetics. My mind is like a sponge when I visit Japan and I have an adventurous palate that's driven by taste, flavour and texture. I'll eat anything. Japan's very important [her export products sell well there] but Italy feeds the soul. It's the place I miss.'

Her personal food philosophy is simple. 'It's all about reacting to produce in its purest form. You need to do so little to really great produce. I have an instinct, never had a lesson in cooking and never used anyone's cookbook. All I did was use smell and touch and taste.'

When I set out to write this book, my aim was to celebrate a diverse group of people who, despite being on opposite sides of the world, are bound by a common passion. Driving back to Adelaide, a line of Maggie Beer's, that 'good food and a

love of life are so intertwined', kept going through my head. In just two hours I had visited her home, met her beloved Col and second daughter Ellie, sat at her piano (when Maggie Beer relaxes she loves to sing jazz), admired the quince orchard and the olive groves, seen where she would celebrate her 60th birthday in January 2005, and visited her export kitchen at Tanunda. I had tasted almost every product in the Maggie Beer range and even a few new, secret ones. I didn't know quite how much of it was captured on my tape, but I knew that if ever I needed reassuring that there was passion in the world, I had only to recall Maggie Beer.

'There are more ideas in my head than I will ever have time to do. At our last strategy meeting there were 115 ideas. Yes, I've major ambitions left but I'm incredibly content with what I've done. The great thing about life is that it just never stops.'

'Every time I serve this roast chook, guests marvel at the flavour and texture, which have less to do with the recipe than with the quality of this well-brought-up chicken. It's so incredibly different from a mass-produced bird that you'd wonder whether they were the same species.'

chook roasted with garlic and verjuice

30 cloves garlic, unpeeled
1 lemon
one 2.5 kg (5 lb 8 oz) free-range chicken (Barossa chook or similar quality)
3 sprigs rosemary
sea salt
freshly ground black pepper
300 ml (10½ fl oz) verjuice
50 ml (1½ fl oz) extra virgin olive oil

Preheat the oven to 220° C (425°F/Gas 7). Blanch the garlic in boiling water for 1 minute, then drain.

Cut the lemon in half and squeeze the juice into the cavity of the chicken, then add the rosemary and season with salt and pepper. Mix 50 ml (1½ fl oz) verjuice with the olive oil and some salt and pepper, then brush this over the skin of the bird. Sit the chook on a trivet in a shallow roasting tin (about 5 cm/2 inches deep), then transfer to the middle shelf of the oven and cook for 20 minutes.

Reduce the oven temperature to 180° C (350° F/Gas 4) and pour 125 ml (4 fl oz/½ cup) of the verjuice and 125 ml (4 fl oz/½ cup) water over the chicken. Put the blanched garlic into the bottom of the roasting tin. Cook for another 20 minutes, then reduce the oven temperature to 120° C (235° F/Gas 1) and add another 125 ml verjuice and 125 ml water (doing this stops the juices burning in the baking dish). Cook for another 20 minutes, then turn the chook over to brown the underside for 10 minutes. Remove the chook to a warm serving plate and cover with foil, then allow to rest for 25 minutes.

Pour all the juices in the baking dish into a tall, narrow pitcher, then refrigerate this while the chicken is resting. Just before serving, scoop away the fat that has risen to the top, then warm the remaining jus, reducing it if need be. Carve the chook, then pour over the jus and serve with the roasted garlic, boiled waxy potatoes and a bitter green salad.

Serves 6

'These cooking times are approximate. Domestic ovens vary greatly in their ability to heat evenly and to recover the heat once the door has been opened. The breast should feel firm and yet yield to a soft squeeze when it is ready.'

roasted pheasant with sage, orange and juniper berries

one 1 kg (2 lb 4 oz) pheasant
1 orange
125 ml (4 fl oz/½ cup) extra virgin olive oil
20 juniper berries, bruised
2 teaspoons chopped fresh marjoram
2 teaspoons chopped fresh thyme
freshly ground black pepper
½ cup loosely packed sage leaves
50 g (1½ oz) butter
125 ml (4 fl oz/½ cup) reduced chicken stock, warmed
125 ml (4 fl oz/½ cup) verjuice
sea salt

Cut the legs away from the pheasant, then cut up either side of the backbone and discard it. 'Spatchcock' the bird by flattening it out. Remove the zest from half the orange with a potato peeler, then juice the orange. Roughly chop the zest and reserve. In a non-metallic dish, marinate the pheasant in the orange juice, olive oil, juniper berries, marjoram, thyme and pepper for 1–4 hours.

Preheat the oven to 200° C (400° F/Gas 6). Remove the stalks from the sage, if desired, then spread the leaves out on a baking tray and dot with the butter. Bake for 12 minutes, until crisp and nut-brown, then set aside. Increase the oven temperature to 230° C (450° F/Gas 8).

Put the pheasant legs and flattened-out breast into a shallow roasting tin, skin side up, and scatter the marinade ingredients around the bird. Season with salt.

Roast the pheasant for 12 minutes, then reduce the temperature to 180° C (350° F/Gas 4)and cook for a further 10 minutes. Remove the legs from the roasting tin, cover and keep warm, then turn the breast over and return it to the oven for a further 2 minutes. Check the bird is cooked by inserting a skewer into the meatiest part — if the juices run clear, the bird is ready. Remove from the oven and add the warmed chicken stock, the verjuice and the remaining butter to the roasting tin. Rest the pheasant, breast down, for at least 10 minutes.

Carve the breast away from the bone and serve with the cooked leg, drizzled with the jus and topped with the crisped sage leaves and chopped orange zest. Serve with braised witlof and a salad of radicchio, rocket (arugula), fennel and walnuts.

Serves 2

Above: roasted pheasant with sage, orange and juniper berries
Opposite: fig galette

maggie beer

'This is a pie I served in Paris for the Baudin Exhibition in 2001. I needed to make 600 small cocktail pies for the occasion and wanted something intrinsically Australian — so what better than this?'

kangaroo tail pie

1 large onion, roughly chopped
1 carrot, roughly chopped
1 clove garlic, roughly chopped
extra virgin olive oil
2 kangaroo tails, approximately
1.5 kg (3 lb 5 oz) total, each cut
into 3 pieces
seasoned plain (all-purpose) flour
500 ml (17 fl oz/2 cups) veal stock
or jellied golden chicken stock
6 lemon myrtle leaves
375 ml (13 fl oz/1½ cups) red wine
sea salt and ground black pepper

pastry
1 packet Tandaco suet mix (believe
me, it works and is terrific!)
250 g (9 oz/2 cups) plain
(all-purpose) flour
250 ml (9 fl oz/1 cup) water
1½ teaspoons baking powder
cracked native pepper

to finish the pie filling
75 g (²⁄₃ cup) diced shallots
70 g (½ cup) diced celery
50 g (⅓ cup) diced carrot
2 tablespoons extra virgin olive oil

Preheat the oven to 140° C (275°F/Gas 1). Choose a heavy-based pot that can be covered (otherwise, put foil on top). Seal the onion, carrot and garlic in extra virgin olive oil, then remove and set aside.

Dust the roo pieces in the seasoned flour and gently seal in the cooking pot. Add half the stock, the sealed vegetables and the lemon myrtle leaves. Deglaze the pot with the red wine, then add the remainder of the stock. Cover and put in the oven for 1½ hours. Turn the tails and continue cooking until tender. Total cooking time will be about 3½ hours, although it could be more for larger pieces of tail and less for the ends of the tails.

Rest the roo to room temperature, then take the meat off the bone and dice it. Two whole tails (1.5 kg/3 lb 5 oz raw weight) should yield 550 g (1 lb 4 oz) meat. Strain the cooking liquid and set aside.

For the pastry, combine all the ingredients and work until smooth and uniform, wrap and rest for 1 hour at room temperature.

Sauté the mirepoix in the oil then add the cooking liquid and reduce a little. Season well, add to the chopped meat and check seasoning.

Take 25 g (1 oz) of pastry and roll into a circle about 8 cm (3½ inches) in diameter and as thin as 1–1.5 mm (¹⁄₂₄–¹⁄₁₆ inch). Fill generously with 1½ tablespoons meat mixture. Fold into a turnover shape, glaze with milk and bake at 180° C (350° F/Gas 4) for 15 minutes.

Makes about 40

*'Autumn is the richest time for all the foods
I love the most. Of all the fruits I have to choose
from, it's a toss-up between quince, pomegranate,
persimmons and figs, but it's my sentimental
attachment to my burnt fig jam that wins out
here. That bitter edge of the "purposely burnt jam"
is the legacy of my Mother's only attempt ever at
jam making and the memory of her wonderfully
distracted style that I still miss today.'*

fig galette

rough puff pastry
450 g (1 lb) unbleached plain
(all-purpose) flour
450 g (1 lb) chilled unsalted butter,
diced
1/2 teaspoon salt
250 ml (9 fl oz/1 cup) cold water

180 g (6 1/4 oz) Maggie's burnt fig jam
8 large, ripe black figs

To make the pastry, tip the flour onto a bench and make a well in the centre. Put the diced butter and the salt into the well, then, using a pastry scraper, cut the butter into the flour. Make a well again and pour in 185 ml (6 fl oz/3/4 cup) of the cold water. Using the pastry scraper, work the flour and butter into the water, adding the remaining water if necessary, to make a firm but pliable dough. Gather the pastry into a ball, then cut this in half and gently pat each piece into a disc and wrap it in plastic wrap. Refrigerate one piece of pastry for 20 minutes. Date the other and put it into the freezer for next time you're making a galette or need rough puff.

Roll the pastry out to make a rectangle about 1.5 cm (5/8 inch) thick. Keeping the longer side of the rectangle parallel to the bench, fold both ends into the centre — it will look like an open book. Then fold one side over the other as though closing the book. Cover and refrigerate the pastry again for 20 minutes. Repeat this step twice.

Preheat the oven to 200° C (400° F/Gas 6). Roll out the pastry to make a round 30–35 cm (12–14 inches) in diameter and about 5 mm (1/4 inch) thick. Spread the fig jam over the pastry. Thickly slice the figs and arrange these on the pastry in overlapping concentric circles, leaving a 5 cm (2 inch) border. Gently fold the pastry border over the figs. Bake the galette for 25–30 minutes, until the pastry is golden brown and the figs are just cooked.

Serves 8–10

antonio and priscilla carluccio

It was a stroke of genius to visit London in October. Lunch with the Carluccios at their Neal Street Restaurant during the fleeting white truffle season. Sheer coincidence of course, but what a nice one. Over lunch, Priscilla Carluccio mentions casually that this season the white truffles from Alba, in Italy's Piedmont region, are worth £3600 per kilo (approximately $AUD9000), and as one does, I'm trying to estimate the value of the shavings on my plate — in fact on each bite — of *uova di quaglia al tartufo bianco d'alba*, a buttery dish of baked quail eggs prepared as a perfect foil for the mighty *tartufo*. 'You can give him a decent lot because he's starved of white truffle in Australia', instructs Priscilla, as Antonio shaves the fungus on to my plate.

She's right, of course. 'We lent one of these out to a magazine the other day,' she laughs. 'I said, "You do realise these are as valuable as diamonds?".' As it turns out, the hapless magazine obviously didn't know, returned the truffle in a sorry state and had to pay up. It would have weighed hardly anything, but even so, I'm thinking of the magazine's poor budget.

A catch-up with the Carluccios is always a pleasure. Each time we meet, the business they preside over seems to have doubled in size. Their smart Carluccio's cafés (offspring of their long-established Neal Street Restaurant and Carluccio's provedore in London's Covent Garden), scattered across London and throughout the south-east of England, are the perfect hybrid of Priscilla's shrewdly creative business acumen and Antonio's passionate flamboyance. The Italian restaurateur made his home in Britain thirty years ago but will forever be the warm, fuzzy Italian from central casting to a generation of Brits familiar with his BBC television series and shelf of best-selling cookbooks. They love him.

I first met the Carluccios in 1998. Antonio was in my sights as a potential contributor for *Food Illustrated* and his generosity and obvious passion for regional Italian food made for a memorable lunch, but it was Priscilla who impressed on that particular day. The sister of Sir Terence Conran, she trained as a photographer and was once the stylist for the influential British Habitat stores and buying director for The Conran Shop. Priscilla Carluccio is a commanding woman, with the sharp Conran eye and an intellect to match. Like her brother, you sense she doesn't suffer fools, but there's warmth, depth and a great sense of humour. After our lunch I realised it was Priscilla who should write for the magazine. Hers was a voice that hadn't been heard.

'That was exciting,' she recalls. '*Food Illustrated* was the first magazine ever to ask me to write. I was quite nervous but I took it as a big compliment.' Priscilla's columns revealed the intense love of Italian flavours that she shares with her husband. 'With a name like Carluccio people always expect me to be Italian,' she wrote. 'But as a matter of fact I don't have any difficulty in borrowing the nationality. The journey through the regional gastronomy of Italy is long, lavish and full of passion. And it is a journey I am very glad to be making.'

That journey, of course, has always been made with Antonio. When they met, Carluccio, was managing the Neal Street Restaurant in Covent Garden for Terence Conran. When he arrived in London in the mid-1970s, Italian food still meant avocado pear and *gamberetti*, *pollo surprese*, and caramelized oranges. 'Some of the trattoria were very good,' he recalls, 'but I still remember restaurateurs who borrowed menus from other restaurateurs when they opened.'

In 1985, Carluccio bought The Neal Street Restaurant from Conran, and for twenty years it has won plaudits as one of Britain's finest Italian restaurants. It now sits as the flagship of the Carluccio empire. Ask Carluccio what his, and the restaurant's, philosophy is and he replies mysteriously, 'Mof-mof!' — which turns out to be Carluccio-speak for 'minimum of fuss, maximum of flavour'. It's a maxim that has served him well. Scanning the menu, he lights on some favourite dishes. A porcini mushroom soup, pan-fried *foie gras*, calf's liver and sweetbread with onions and spinach. Robust food.

'I am a purist,' he explains. 'I was never keen to know about *nouvelle cuisine* because I knew I didn't like it. It was embellishment for the sake of embellishment. For me food has to have a function.'

There is a popular misconception that Carluccio is a trained chef. He is — quite emphatically — not. 'I was never a chef, I am a cook. I cook for passion or greed or whatever you like, but in private. I never became professional, I don't like to cook under pressure. I am simply a cook and a restaurateur who is interested in food. I read about it, I write about it …' A quick study of the Neal Street menu will also reveal his great passion, mushrooms. There's *trifolata di funghi del giorno* (mushrooms of the day), the *zuppa di porcini*, the *prosciutto crudo di parma* served with preserved mushrooms, gnocchi with a wild boar and mushroom *ragu*, and baked partridge served with wild mushrooms. Carluccio's romance with funghi produced his famous mushroom book that has since been published in nine countries and almost as many languages. 'When you smell the rotting wood and then you smell the mushroom, you know you are truly in the middle of nature', he explains, with the beatific smile of the truly rapt. 'When you experience something like that from the earth you can't be anything other than happy.'

The Carluccios have worked together for a long time. Their legendary Neal Street food store (one of the first London provedores to sell genuine, meticulously-sourced Italian produce) adjacent to the restaurant, was opened in 1991. They must obviously share a very successful personal formula. Antonio excuses himself to take a call and I ask Priscilla about the Carluccio chemistry. 'It's hugely difficult working together, hell really', she laughs, wide-eyed at my suggestion it might be otherwise. 'I think anybody who's honest would say it's hell, but we just happen to have these two separate paths that actually, when they go together, make an interesting whole. But I would never recommend a husband and wife working together, I think it's a terrible idea.' She reflects for a second. 'Well, maybe from a business point of view it's okay. I think that people who scream and shout at each other usually create a dynamic that's quite good. It's uncomfortable to live with it but it's gutsy!'

The Carluccios have seen plenty of changes in British food and in Italian food in Britain. There are doubtless still plenty of trattorias serving *pollo surprese*, but surely things are better? Priscilla agrees. 'There's a genuine interest again in food and thank god it's back. I think that after the two world wars food became very scarce. And then we became very excited about foreign food, obviously because we had been starved of anything else, so I think the time for British food has come back. It's very exciting.'

She and Antonio (like so many of the people I met in London in 2004) claim Fergus Henderson of London's St John restaurant as the saviour of modern British food. 'Fergus is my hero', admits Antonio. 'I take my hat off to him', adds Priscilla. 'I think he's probably done more than anybody for British food.' On the Italian scene ('if we have to choose another Italian') they are unanimous that Giorgio Locatelli 'can really cook'.

So if Antonio is the cook in this relationship, what about Priscilla? How does she define her role. The eyes sparkle. 'Bossy!' she says without a moment's hesitation, and funnily enough, I don't doubt her. I just hope that one day she will write again.

baked mushroom bruschetta

300 g (10½ oz) mushrooms of
your choice
55 g (2 oz/¼ cup) butter
4 tablespoons olive oil
1 clove garlic, finely chopped
1 small fresh red chilli, finely
chopped
juice of half a lemon
1 tablespoon finely chopped
flat-leaf (Italian) parsley
185 ml (6 fl oz/¾ cup) thick
(double/heavy) cream
4 large slices Italian country bread,
toasted on both sides
100 g (3½ oz/⅔ cup) taleggio
or mozzarella cheese,
cut into chunks
55 g (2 oz/⅔ cup) fresh breadcrumbs
salt and pepper, to taste

Preheat the oven to 230° C (450° F/Gas 8), or preheat the grill (broiler).

Clean and trim the mushrooms as appropriate, and cut the large ones into pieces if necessary. Sauté the mushrooms in the butter and oil, with the garlic and chilli, until slightly softened. Add the lemon juice and parsley and stir briefly. Add the cream and cook for about 10 minutes, or until the mushrooms are tender. Season to taste.

Top each slice of toast with some of the mixture and dot with the cheese. Sprinkle with the breadcrumbs and bake or grill (broil) for 5 minutes, or until the cheese is bubbling. Serve immediately.

Serves 4

truffled quails with balsamic sauce

stuffing
55 g (2 oz/²/₃ cup) fresh breadcrumbs
50 g (1³/₄ oz/¹/₂ cup) grated
parmesan cheese
1 tablespoon finely chopped
flat-leaf (Italian) parsley
1 egg
50 g (1³/₄ oz) mortadella,
finely cubed
¹/₂ teaspoon truffle oil
salt and pepper, to taste

4 partly boned small quails
8 slices pancetta
olive oil, for frying

sauce
150 ml (5 fl oz) saba (see note)
50 g (1³/₄ oz) butter
2 tablespoons brandy

For the stuffing, mix together the breadcrumbs, parmesan cheese, parsley, egg, mortadella, truffle oil and salt and pepper to taste. Stuff the quails with the mixture, wrap the pancetta slices around them and secure with a toothpick.

To cook the quails, gently fry them in a little olive oil for 15 minutes, then put in a hot oven for a further 10 minutes. In another pan, gently cook the saba with the butter and brandy. Remove the quails from the oven and place in the pan with the saba sauce, spooning the sauce over the birds. Serve hot with braised savoy cabbage and sautéed potatoes.

Serves 4

Note: Saba is a cooked, reduced grape juice, available from Italian food stores and delicatessens.

spaghettini with tomato sauce

90 ml (3 fl oz) extra virgin olive oil
2 cloves garlic, crushed
1 kg (2 lb 4 oz) ripe tomatoes,
peeled, deseeded and chopped
600 g (1 lb 5 oz) spaghettini
6 basil leaves, plus extra to serve
salt and pepper

Heat the oil in a pan and gently fry the garlic for a few minutes without allowing it to colour. Add the tomatoes and fry, stirring constantly, for 5 minutes, allowing just the excess liquid to evaporate.

Cook the pasta in boiling salted water until *al dente*, add the basil to the sauce, then mix half of the sauce with the pasta.

Divide among serving plates and spoon the remaining sauce on top of the pasta along with more basil leaves. Cheese is optional, but I wouldn't use it.

Serves 6

zabaglione with muscatel

4 medium egg yolks
110 g (scant 4 oz) caster (superfine)
sugar
175 ml (6 fl oz) Moscato Passito

Beat the egg yolks with the sugar until the sugar is dissolved. Add the wine and beat for a few minutes more. Put in a bain-marie over a low heat and, using a whisk, beat until a firm, foamy consistency is obtained. This will take 5–10 minutes, depending on the freshness of the eggs and on the heat. Take care not to overcook it and turn it into scrambled eggs! Spoon into individual glasses and serve with very delicately flavoured biscuits.

Serves 4

Late in 1998, Stephanie Alexander — chef, author and all-round national food treasure — and fellow food writer Maggie Beer were in London to promote the beautiful *Tuscan Cookbook* they had co-written. A lunch, hosted in their honour by Nigella Lawson, was diverted at the last moment to the home of author Claudia Roden, due, I believe, to the sadly deteriorating condition of Lawson's late husband, the journalist John Diamond. It was a wonderful lunch, both poignant and celebratory, Beer and Alexander seducing us with their big Australian personalities and passionate tales of Tuscany. I remember being entranced by Lawson (commanding and regal even then, in her pre-domestic goddess days) and captivated by the largesse of the two Australian women.

stephanie alexander

A few days later, I interviewed Stephanie and Maggie at our west London offices for a profile in *Food Illustrated*. The taxi that was booked to take them to their hotel didn't show, so they were bundled into my car and shunted along Bayswater Road at the obligatory snail's pace. As we crawled along in the dark, immobilized and dispirited (me that is, not Stephanie and Maggie, who were perfectly chirpy) by the rush-hour traffic and a steady downpour, I made my decision to move to Australia, where there would surely never be traffic jams and taxis would arrive on time. Naïvety is a wonderful thing. The profile was never written, as I promptly turned my life upside down and left the magazine in preparation for my move. Stephanie and Maggie, I hope I have now made amends.

For 21 years, until its closure in 1997, Stephanie Alexander ran the legendary Stephanie's restaurant in Melbourne. Sadly for me, I never got to eat there, arriving too late on Australian shores (if I were allowed just two days of time travel, I would flip back first to Stephanie's and then to Gay Bilson's celebrated Berowra Waters Inn) but anecdotally, the influence of Stephanie's restaurant and its lauded

chef–proprietor was obviously remarkable, leaving an indelible stamp on the food culture of Australia.

'I have a very strong tendency to repeat my life', muses Alexander over a cup of tea in her comfortable Melbourne kitchen. We are talking about her present successful business, where I had just enjoyed a delicious lunch. 'The Richmond Hill Café and Larder was devised as a fun place I could just drift into and sit around and have a cup of coffee or a glass of wine, but it's become big business and I've taken on some of the stress again, though this time not on my own.' There's a tremor of resignation in the admission that Alexander 'could almost contemplate life without a restaurant', but the 'almost' in that sentence is telling. One senses there are still a great many challenges left in her.

When *Food Illustrated* published its list of the greatest cookbooks of all time, Stephanie Alexander's *The Cook's Companion* was amongst them. 'Alexander is an Australian institution,' they wrote, 'and this is her magnum opus.' It's a seminal work for which Alexander has received justifiable acclaim in Australia and overseas. Vast and comprehensive, the original version, published in 1996, ran to more than 800 pages, and took almost three years to write and a further year to edit. She is pragmatic about the book's success. 'The fact that 300,000 people bought it, let alone how many others were influenced by it, borrowed it from their mother or got it from the library, represents a real need for straightforward, simple information that didn't muck around and got down to the nitty gritty.' In 2004, a revised edition of *The Cook's Companion* was published with an additional 300 pages, new chapters and hundreds of new recipes, acknowledging the changes in Australian food over a period of almost ten years.

Stephanie Alexander would probably consider it a compliment if I say that her food is neither directional nor cutting-edge. It is simply good food, Stephanie's

food. 'I still think I can recognise good food when I find it, whether it be a smart new idea or a beautiful rabbit stew. There's a practical element to what I do. It's about being alive, having a life, needing to go to four meetings and deal with emails. Food is part of my life, it blends in, it's not up on a pedestal.'

'Good food in restaurants', she continues, 'exists in the hand of someone who really understands food. The most satisfying dishes are where the food has got some point. A good cook knows the bread to use for a good sandwich.'

Alexander often credits her late mother as her mentor, but there have been other influences, such as regular travels in her beloved Italy and France and 'great writers' such as the late Richard Olney, Claudia Roden and Marcella Hazan. She tempers her praise for Elizabeth David with an observation. 'I think she was probably a horror,' she laughs, 'but she wrote beautiful prose and evoked some wonderful things. She is very sensual in the pictures she paints of things, that extraordinary ability to get to the essence of a dish in about three lines.'

While I was writing this book, it amused me to read an interview with Alexander in *Australian Country Style* magazine in which she admitted to being 'quite fierce as a girl, very wilful and quite bossy'. That's kind of how I'd always viewed the adult Stephanie Alexander. Determined, passionate, feisty, no-nonsense. Yes, perhaps a little bossy. Quite intimidating. But the stern demeanour (which she might have acquired in her well-documented early career as a librarian) softens frequently into laughter, and there's a sharp sense of humour. When I point out the polarity of the current obsession with fast-assembly food (as in *Donna Hay Magazine* readers) and the rising popularity of the Slow Food movement in Australia, Alexander replies: 'If you added those two groups together you've probably got about one per cent of the population. Then there's the other ninety-nine per cent who couldn't give a shit.' She's right, of course. Sometimes magazine editors need a reality check.

Despite the success of *The Cook's Companion* and ten other acclaimed cookbooks, she is still reluctant to call herself a food writer. 'I think there's a feeling out there in the writing community that food is a frivolous, effete interest.' She is nevertheless happy to call herself a 'food activist'. Since 2001, much of Alexander's energies have been directed to the Collingwood Kitchen Garden Project, which encourages schoolkids in an inner-city Melbourne suburb to enjoy food, from the ground up. 'Some children live on takeaway or microwaved food ... it's really quite scary. Very few of them ever eat with anybody and they're not in the habit of seeing eating as a social activity or eating food that has started out as fresh ingredients. Each week the kids [130 of them between the ages of seven and eleven] spend forty minutes in the garden and eighty minutes in the kitchen. It's a committed part of the school curriculum.'

'Food is part of life,' she continues, 'but let's make it a fantastically rich part of life. It's essential that we do not talk to the children about health or nutrition — ever. It's about enjoyable, positive experiences and just having a fantastic time. We never say this is protein, this is carbohydrate and you should restrict your intake of fat.' Some might be aghast at such apparent irresponsibility, but I believe Alexander is right. In a society that often views dinner as something eaten alone in front of a television screen, probably processed, isn't it fantastic to get kids growing, talking, cooking, feeling and sharing the beauty of good food. Nor would it be on Alexander's agenda anyway to provide anything that is less than simple, seasonal and nutritious. 'Every other cultural group I can think of — India, the Middle East, China, all of Asia and the Mediterranean countries — they all eat well and know that everything else can be wrong in life but you can always eat good food.'

It's a corny question but I always love to know the answer. What would Stephanie Alexander have done if she hadn't made a career from food? 'I'd probably still be in a library, still cooking madly for my friends.' She looks thoughtful. 'For me the greatest pleasure is cooking for people — usually very old friends — who happily luxuriate in the knowledge that I love to cook for them. They always wash the dishes and we talk. They're always the happiest times.'

'Now that one can buy duck breasts in the market, what used to be a restaurant-only dish is possible at home.'

grilled duck breast

2 potatoes
2 boneless duck breasts, skin on
1 teaspoon salt
freshly ground black pepper
1 tablespoon olive oil or rendered duck fat
2 large flat mushrooms, thickly sliced
1 clove garlic, finely chopped
2 tablespoons freshly chopped flat-leaf (Italian) parsley

Boil the potatoes in their skins, then peel and cut into bite-sized pieces. Set aside.

Preheat the oven to 120° C (235°F/Gas 1). With a sharp knife, score the duck skin deeply in a criss-cross pattern. Rub the skin with salt and pepper. Heat a heavy-based frying pan, add the oil and place the duck breasts in the pan, skin side down. Adjust the heat so there is a good sizzle but no suggestion of scorching. Cook for 6–8 minutes, then pour any accumulated fat into a small bowl. Turn the duck breasts and cook for 1–2 minutes on the flesh side. Wrap loosely in foil and place, skin-side down, on a plate in the oven to keep warm.

Return the duck fat to the pan and sauté the reserved potato for 5 minutes until a bit crusty around the edges. Add the mushrooms and, still with heat fairly high, toss all together. Scatter over the garlic and parsley, shake once more and turn off the heat.

Remove the duck from the oven and cut into thinnish slices on an angle. Arrange on plates and add the potato and mushrooms. Serve with a green salad.

Serves 2

'The name of this dish came about because the combination of eggs cooked in butter with cumin, lemon and mint is popular in Iraq.'

baghdad eggs

20 g (³/₄ oz) butter
1 clove garlic, finely sliced
1 tablespoon lemon juice
2 eggs
freshly ground cumin seeds
1 slice hot toast or 1 flatbread
salt
freshly ground black pepper
a few shredded mint leaves

Melt the butter and, when it starts to foam, drop in the garlic. Cook for 30 seconds, until just starting to change colour. Add the lemon juice and eggs and fry gently until set.

Sprinkle over a good pinch of cumin and serve on toast or flatbread. Season with salt, pepper and mint.

Serves 1

Opposite: squid with bronze skin
Above: queen of nuts cake with braised peaches

squid with bronze skin

4 squid, bodies about 15 cm
(6 inches) long
4 cloves garlic
freshly ground black pepper
(or 1 long hot chilli, seeded
and sliced)
enough extra virgin olive oil
to half cover the squid
when packed into a dish

Clean the squid but do not skin. Leave the tentacles in one piece. Slice the garlic finely. Put the squid, garlic, black pepper (or chilli) and oil in a shallow dish for several hours, turning once or twice.

Prepare a bed of glowing coals (or heat a barbecue grill). Lift the squid from the dish and drain in a colander over a plate to remove excess oil, which would flare up on the grill. Place the bodies and tentacles over the coals or on to the barbecue. Grill for 4–5 minutes per side, or until the tip of a small knife or a skewer can pass through the body quite easily. The skin will have developed marvellous bronze markings. Transfer the squid to a warm dish and spoon over a little of the olive oil from the marinade. Rest for 5 minutes. Squeeze over fresh lemon juice if you want.

Slice thinly and serve just as it is, with salad leaves or over delicate pasta. You probably won't need any salt, but check.

Serves 4

'A great favourite. I cannot remember where the recipe came from but I have been making it for years. It needs a light hand with the mixing, and do not overbeat the egg whites. Whether you use blanched or unblanched almonds is up to you. For the braised peaches, we use the amarone-style wine produced by Jo and Diane Grilli at their Primo Estate winery in South Australia's Barossa Valley. The vines are double-pruned and the fruit is picked late, concentrating its flavour.'

queen of nuts cake with braised peaches

20 g (³/₄ oz) butter, melted
2 tablespoons fine breadcrumbs
200 g (7 oz) best-quality bittersweet chocolate, broken into pieces
150 g (5¹/₂ oz/1¹/₂ cups) unblanched or blanched ground almonds
145 g (5 oz/²/₃ cup) caster (superfine) sugar
30 g (1 oz) candied citron or other moist candied peel, minced
5 eggs, separated
2 drops vanilla extract

braised peaches
80 g (2³/₄ oz) unsalted butter
8 large yellow peaches, perfectly ripe, peeled and cut in half
4 tablespoons sugar
2 lemon myrtle leaves
600 ml (21 fl oz) red wine

Preheat the oven to 160° C (315° F/Gas 2–3). Line the base of a 22 cm (8¹/₂ inch) round cake tin with baking (parchment) paper. Brush the paper and the sides of the tin with melted butter, then tip in the breadcrumbs and turn to coat the buttered surfaces. Tap to remove any excess. Line 2 baking trays with foil. Roughly grate the chocolate in a food processor (a bit of texture is good — do not process it to chocolate dust) and tip into a large bowl. Add the ground almonds, sugar and citron and mix lightly but well. In a separate bowl, whisk egg yolks lightly with vanilla, then stir into the chocolate mixture.

Beat the egg whites until they are satiny with creamy, soft peaks. Using a flexible plastic scraper, fold a third of the egg white into the chocolate mixture. Gently fold in the remaining egg white in 2 batches. Spoon batter into cake tin and bake for about 40 minutes, or until cake feels firm in the centre (a skewer inserted into the cake will still be moist because of the chocolate). Cool in tin, away from draughts, for 15 minutes, then turn out onto one of the prepared trays. Turn right-side up onto the other tray and cool completely.

For the braised peaches, melt the butter in an enamelled cast-iron frying pan large enough to hold all the peaches in one layer. When melted and the foam has subsided, place the peaches, cut side down, to colour lightly. Scatter over the sugar and lemon myrtle leaves. Adjust heat so that the butter and sugar start to form a caramel syrup, but don't burn. Gently shake the pan to prevent the peaches sticking. After 2 minutes, turn the peaches using a flexible spatula. Add half the wine. It should bubble vigorously around the fruit. Add the rest of the wine and gently shake the pan again to assist the blending of the wine, caramel and juices from the fruit. The peaches will be ready in about 5 minutes. They are delicious hot or warm, and one does not have to make the cake at all. When cold, the butter congeals and the peaches do not look wonderful, but a quick re-warming in their juices remedies this.

Serves 8

What a fuss about a ponytail. Shortly after I arrived in Sydney, the city's chefs and restaurateurs were up in arms over a remark made in print by a *Sydney Morning Herald* journalist over the supposed 'limp' state of chef Neil Perry's ponytail after his celebrated Rockpool restaurant lost a chef's hat — akin to a star Michelin star — in the *Herald*'s annual *Good Food Guide*. It was admittedly a catty remark (and illogical too — isn't a ponytail by its very nature limp?), but I found the controversy that raged around it astonishing.

neil perry

With hindsight, the remark had simply ignited the powder keg that was the food community's frustration over the power of the *Good Food Guide*. The loss of Rockpool's chef's hat — long since redeemed — had upset the status quo, and Perry's ponytail was simply emblematic of a deeper malaise. But to a new boy in town, the incident demonstrated just how seriously Sydney takes its food, how brittle are the egos of some if its stars (nothing new there) and importantly, the venerable status of Neil Perry, ponytail and all, within the city's close-knit food community.

In 1998, Perry's high-profile relationship with Australian national airline Qantas was in its infancy and the chef was in London to promote the airline's new business-class service. I interviewed him for *Food Illustrated*, and remember his black leather jacket, the aforementioned ponytail and a flash-trash Gloucester Road hotel suite that made it all feel very rock-and-roll. Like most British food editors, I was familiar with Perry through his regular appearances in the Australian magazines to which we all subscribed (a sad indictment on our British publications of the time is that the most eagerly anticipated bi-monthly event was the arrival of the new issue of *Vogue Entertaining + Travel*). Neil Perry embodied the cool modernity of Australian food, and I wanted the story direct from the source. Instead, there was a tiresome PR person hell-bent on ensuring that nothing much of interest was discussed, and I recall too that Perry was jet-lagged, though that could have been the PR person's ruse to keep our lack of conversation moving swiftly along.

The next time I place a microphone in front of him, in August 2004, things are different. It's just us, give or take the odd nagging mobile phone, but at least there's no pressure to discuss airline seats. Our early morning conversation is at Rockpool, his landmark restaurant in The Rocks district of Sydney, and probably Australia's most famous restaurant. Perry is a man at the top of his profession and on top of the world. He is putting the finishing touches to his third book, he is two weeks away from opening a new Asian restaurant in the inner city, and most importantly, he has a new four-week-old daughter, Macy, by his third wife, Sam (Perry also has an eleven-year-old daughter, Josephine). He has every reason to be a happy man, but he also has every reason to be a knackered one. He looks infuriatingly good.

Perry is neither modest nor boastful. He is simply upfront about his personal achievements and those of Rockpool. He has a lot to be proud of and he's worked bloody hard for it. Perry is a passionate ambassador for the food of his country, both within Australia and internationally, and has raised the bar for the restaurant industry. He is still the best-known Australian chef outside Australia, which is remarkable given that all of his business ventures to date have been on home soil. Australians are familiar with his face on television (he has made seven series for the Australian Lifestyle Channel, which screen in more than 55 countries), and in their supermarkets. Perry has an exclusive range at Woolworths supermarkets in Australia. 'We've got a product on the shelves there that's unique and better than anything else in the super-market' is a typical Perry claim, but you don't doubt the truth of it.

And on the day I'm writing this, Perry's name is in the newspaper along with those of fellow Australians Nicole Kidman, Mel Gibson, Cate Blanchett and Geoffrey Rush, all of whom have been honoured at a lavish Australia Day banquet in Los Angeles. Australian actors are the current flavour of Hollywood, and of course Perry is there to bring them a taste of home. For the second year running, he is behind the stoves preparing Australian produce that has been flown across the Pacific for the 1200 guests. Fresh yabbies, hiramasa kingfish, Western Australian lobsters, Victorian lamb ...

'I'm one of the only Australian-born guys to have hit the top,' he says matter-of-factly, 'and I'm so lucky to be involved in things like Qantas. I'm very proud of that.' Perry's menus for Qantas are exceptional. Having flown backwards and forwards between Australia and Europe for more than a decade, on a variety of airlines, I know my in-flight trays. Believe me.

Perry is an innovator. He considers the Blue Water Grill restaurant that he ran at Sydney's Bondi Beach in the mid-1980s [he started his career waiting tables but crossed to the kitchen in the early 80s] to have changed the direction of food in Sydney. 'It was a casual dining room that was as much about having fun as it was about eating good food. It was really just me grilling fish, throwing it on a plate and the person next to me putting a lump of curry butter on it. There were just thirty things on the menu. People would come up from the beach with sand on their feet, order a glass of wine and a mud crab or a gorgeous piece of tuna. We got people thinking about what modern Australian food was.'

Rockpool, the award-winning fine-dining restaurant that Perry opened in 1989, definitely didn't have sand between its toes. 'Rockpool was to be a world-class restaurant that Australians could be proud of. It was one of the first restaurants to put everything together. Food, wine, service, décor, the total experience. Rockpool was all about going the extra nine yards.' Rockpool was, incidentally, the most expensive restaurant Sydney had ever seen, with a fit-out bill of AUD$1.8 million, no small sum in 1988.

Run your eye over the Rockpool menu and Perry's affinity for Asian flavours is evident. King prawn and coconut cake with a *kimchi* flavoured *congee* sauce, Spring Bay scallops with lemon grass, tea-smoked duck with leek and *gai choy*. He might call his food 'Neil Perry food' — 'a direct relationship to my upbringing and influences' — but it's the Asian influences that have left their mark, the legacy perhaps of the six-year-old Perry sharing mud crab in a Chinese restaurant with his father. His rendition of modern Australian food is a synthesis of both Asian and European sensibilities. 'You can see the heritage of Rockpool's food,' he explains, 'but I think we make it our own. Like our black squid-ink noodles. It was wonderful to sit in Venice and eat squid-ink risotto but then you think about bringing it back to Australia and adding fish sauce, wild green chillies or coriander, flavouring it with things that are probably very foreign to the average Italian.' Not to mention replacing rice with noodles.

Perry is not afraid to admit it hasn't always been smooth sailing. Rockpool has stood the test of time, but there have been some fabulous failures too. 'I guess I'm a graduate of life, I've learnt so much through experience. If we hadn't lived through the dark times we wouldn't be in a position to grow successfully now. You can't know love until you've known heartbreak.'

'I'd still like to build the Rockpool brand and develop XO [his new Asian restaurant] into a brand too. I'd love to do something special in London and keep the relationship growing with Qantas. I'd love to build a great food company with Woolworths so that more Australians can eat better, fresher food. And I don't have a lot of aspirations after that. I'm 48 now, so retirement might be a good aspiration.'

Retirement? Neil Perry? Somehow those two things just don't go together.

'I have been cooking this dish for twenty years. It is unctuous and luscious, and if you like pork fat as much as I do, this will be an all-time favourite. Serve with rice and some steamed Asian greens.'

braised pork hock with dark soy sauce

1 whole fresh pork hock (about 500 g/1 lb 2 oz)
2 teaspoons sugar
1 teaspoon salt
160 ml (5¼ fl oz) dark soy sauce
4 tablespoons vegetable oil
5 red shallots, finely sliced
5 slices ginger
5 cloves garlic, finely sliced
2 tablespoons fermented black beans, pounded
100 g (3½ oz/½ cup) crushed yellow rock sugar
1 stick cassia bark
2 star anise
two 10 cm (5-inch) lengths sugar cane, peeled
1 litre (35 fl oz/4 cups) fresh chicken stock
8 dried shiitake mushrooms, soaked in warm water for 20 minutes and stalks discarded
1 fresh bamboo shoot, finely sliced and blanched (or ½ cup tinned bamboo shoots)
3 spring onions (scallions), cut into 4–5 cm (2 inch) lengths

Put the pork hock into a large pot of cold water and bring to the boil. Discard the boiling liquid and wash the hock to remove any impurities. Dry the hock with kitchen paper and then marinate for 1 hour in the sugar, salt and 2 tablespoons of the dark soy.

Heat the oil in a wok and fry the marinated pork slowly until brown on all sides. Add the shallots, ginger, garlic and black beans and fry for a further minute. Transfer to a snug-fitting pot and add the remaining dark soy, the yellow rock sugar, cassia bark, star anise and sugar cane. Pour in the chicken stock, bring to the boil and simmer gently for 2 hours. Add the shiitake mushrooms and bamboo shoots and simmer gently for a further 30-40 minutes. Finally, add the spring onions and simmer for 5 minutes.

To serve, transfer the meat and other ingredients to a deep, warm bowl and pour over the stock (if necessary, reduce the stock until syrupy).

Serves 4 as part of a shared Asian banquet

'A Rockpool classic, this is a combination of Italian and Thai flavors. It is the darkest, sexiest, most mysterious dish I know. Once you get over eating black, you will never look back.'

stir-fried squid and prawns with squid-ink noodles, speck, chilli and coriander

squid-ink noodles
100 g (3½ oz) plain (all-purpose) flour, plus extra for dusting
a pinch of sea salt
1 whole egg
1 egg yolk
1 teaspoon extra virgin olive oil
1 teaspoon squid ink

extra virgin olive oil
200 g (7 oz) cleaned squid tubes, sliced into ½ cm (¼ inch) strips
2 tablespoons diced speck or smoky bacon
4 raw large king prawns (jumbo shrimp), peeled and minced
1 small green chilli, finely sliced
2 cloves garlic, finely chopped
1 teaspoon squid ink
60 ml (2 fl oz/¼ cup) chicken stock
Thai fish sauce
sea salt
125 g (4½ oz) cherry tomatoes, sliced in half
2 tablespoons coriander (cilantro) leaves
half a lemon

For the noodles, sift the flour into a large bowl or straight onto a clean work surface. Add the salt, whole egg, egg yolk and oil. Mix the squid ink with a little water, stir together and add. Mix the dough together and knead gently, being careful not to over-work it.

Wrap the dough in plastic wrap and rest it for 30 minutes. Once the dough has rested, flour it well and pass it through a pasta machine, keeping the dough well doused in flour each passing. When you have reached the desired thickness, roll the dough up and cut into strips.

Bring a pot of water to the boil and blanch the noodles until *al dente*. Drain well.

Heat a frying pan and add a generous splash of extra virgin olive oil. Add the squid, speck or bacon, prawns, chilli and garlic to the pan and stir quickly. Remove the pan from the heat for a moment, add the noodles and return to the heat. Add the squid ink, chicken stock, a dash of fish sauce and a pinch of salt. Add the cherry tomatoes along with the coriander leaves and toss together well. Taste to check seasoning and finish with a squeeze of lemon juice. Divide among four bowls and serve immediately.

Serves 4

Above: stir-fried squid and prawns with squid-ink noodles, speck, chilli and coriander
Opposite: passionfruit tart

'This salad is about beautiful fresh produce in season. If you cook the crab fresh yourself, you will elevate this dish from very good to sublime. Mud crab also works well with these flavours. Don't, whatever you do, use preserved artichokes; the intense flavour kills the subtlety of the dish. Choose baby artichokes, as they have no choke to remove.'

spanner crab *au naturel* with winter vegetables

4 baby artichokes
200 g (7 oz) baby cabbage leaves, very finely shredded
8 whole almonds, roasted, peeled then finely sliced
extra virgin olive oil
1 tablespoon red wine vinegar
sea salt and freshly ground white pepper
240 g (8$^1/_2$ oz) spanner crab meat
4 teaspoons fresh lemon juice

garlic cream
50 g (1$^3/_4$ oz) peeled garlic
200 ml (7 fl oz) whipping cream
sea salt and freshly ground white pepper, to taste

to assemble
5 g ($^1/_8$ oz) sourdough bread, cut into 5 mm ($^1/_4$ inch) dice
4 cloves garlic, sliced thinly and fried in olive oil
20 g ($^3/_4$ oz) Jerusalem artichoke, peeled, sliced thinly and fried in olive oil

Peel the baby artichokes, slice them finely lengthways and place them in acidulated water to stop them discolouring.

Mix the cabbage and sliced raw artichoke together. Add the sliced almonds and a good splash of extra virgin olive oil, the red wine vinegar, sea salt and pepper to taste.

In a separate bowl, mix the crab with 1 tablespoon extra virgin olive oil, the lemon juice, sea salt and pepper to taste.

To make the garlic cream, boil the garlic till very soft, drain, cool, then mash until very smooth in a mortar with a pestle. Whip the cream to soft peaks. Gently mix the garlic through the whipped cream and season to taste.

To assemble, place a pastry ring on each of four service plates and add the salad. Add the sourdough cubes, garlic chips and Jerusalem artichoke chips, top with the crab then gently remove the pastry ring. Finish with a quenelle of about $^1/_2$ tablespoon garlic cream on top (there will be garlic cream left over). Drizzle with extra virgin olive oil.

Serves 4 as an entrée

'As a young child I would pick passionfruit from the vine in the back yard for my mother's pavlova. This passionfruit tart is a lot more sophisticated, but every bit as Australian. This sweet shortcrust pastry is ideal for making custard and fruit tarts. It can be made in advance and will keep in the refrigerator for a week. It also freezes well. The recipe yields one 28 cm (11¼ inch) tart case or several smaller ones.'

passionfruit tart

sweet shortcrust pastry
250 g (9 oz/2 cups) plain (all-purpose) flour
75 g (2½ oz) unsalted butter, cubed
a pinch of sea salt
90 g (3¼ oz/¾ cup) icing (confectioners') sugar, sifted
55 ml (1¾ oz) milk
2 egg yolks

filling
nine 55 g (2 oz) eggs
350 g (12 oz/1½ cups) caster (superfine) sugar
300 ml (10½ fl oz) thick (double/heavy) cream (45% butterfat)
350 ml (12 fl oz) passionfruit juice, strained

plain (all-purpose) flour, for rolling
a little egg wash, for glazing
icing (confectioners') sugar, to serve

For the pastry, place the flour, butter, salt and icing sugar in a food processor and process for 20 seconds. Add the milk and egg yolks and process for a further 30 seconds until a mass forms. Turn out onto a lightly floured surface and knead lightly for a few moments. Form into a ball, wrap in plastic wrap and refrigerate for 1 hour.

Make the passionfruit filling the day before you wish to bake the tart (resting it helps avoid splitting). Break the eggs into a bowl and whisk. Add the sugar and continue to whisk until well incorporated. While stirring gently, pour in the cream. Add the passionfruit juice and stir until well blended. Cover and refrigerate overnight.

Spray a 26 cm (10½ inch) tart tin with flavorless oil spray. Lightly flour a work surface and roll out the pastry until it is 2 cm (¾ inch) wider than the tart case. Roll the pastry over your rolling pin and gently ease into the tart case, pushing the sides in gently so that it takes the fluting. Rest in the refrigerator for 30 minutes.

Preheat the oven to 180° C (350° F/Gas 4). Line tart case with foil, place rice on the foil and blind bake for 20 minutes. Remove rice and foil, brush tart case with egg wash and cook for 10 minutes more. Remove from oven, lower temperature to 140° C (275° F/Gas 1), and return tart case to oven. With the case sitting in the oven, and using a cup, carefully pour in the passionfruit custard, filling the tart case right to the top. Bake for 40 minutes. Check; the tart should be halfway set but still quite wobbly in the middle. If you take it out too soon, it will not set completely and will run when you cut it; if you leave it in too long, it will set too firmly and lose its elegance.

Remove the tart from the oven, balance it on a cup and remove the sides. Put on a cake rack and, with a palette knife, slide the base off the tart tin. This allows the tart to cool and the pastry to crisp up rather than sweat. Invert the pastry ring back onto the tart to help hold the sides in as it cools and sets. Allow to cool for 1 hour. Carefully cut with a serrated knife, dust with icing sugar and serve.

Serves 8

neil perry

Maybe Alastair Hendy and I were separated at birth. We're the same age, we're both from England's Home Counties and we both claim to have had the most stylish bedrooms on the block as kids. We both studied theatre and cite Terence Conran, *Vogue Entertaining + Travel* and the writing of Nigel Slater as seminal influences on our careers, and both our mothers turned to the wise words of British cookery guru Marguerite Patten for advice in the kitchen. Where we differ is that he claims to have cooked as a child. I just ate.

alastair hendy

Alastair Hendy also claims that when we first met I said, 'Come back and see me when you're famous'. He might just as well throw a 'kid' on to the end of that sentence for good measure. Apparently I said it in a nice way, but unless I was channelling Samuel Goldwyn or Louis B. Meyer at that precise moment, I find it unlikely that I would have been so crass. The mundane truth is that I needed a television chef to front the food pages of a new magazine for the Debenhams store group (this was 1996 or 1997) and Hendy, though a prodigious talent even then, was not a household name. He must have taken me at my word, because he went off and became a first-rate, award-winning author and photographer. Though, as he admits himself — with dry humour — the television cameras have yet to love him.

Chatting over coffee at the sleek, industrial warehouse in east London's Shoreditch which serves as the home he shares with his partner, plus studio, office and test kitchen, Hendy (in a conversation punctuated by a ceaselessly demanding phone) tells me 'there isn't a word yet invented' to describe him. He is a human magazine — traveller, writer, cook, food stylist, photographer, art director.

'Are you a control freak, Alastair?'

'Yes, you know I am.'

I certainly do. Talents like Hendy and his Australian counterpart Donna Hay (they may both baulk at the comparison, but I believe they share a similar aesthetic and have both similarly influenced food media in their respective countries) can occasionally be an editor's nightmare because they prefer to do everything their way. Hendy and I have sparred — for the most part good-naturedly — over the years, but he knows I have always respected his talent. As a food stylist, his images gave sophistication and edge to *Food Illustrated*, while his atmospheric travel photographs continue to add magic to the pages of *Vogue Entertaining + Travel*.

Hendy's career has been a cocktail of talent and amazing good fortune. An antique dealer with a passion for food, he met Antonio Carluccio (the Carluccios are friends and an enduring presence in his career) through a BBC Good Food magazine cooking competition (Carluccio was a judge) which he didn't win. Not one to be deterred, Hendy then put himself through the gruelling paces of BBC TV's *Masterchef*. Again, he didn't win, but the experience gave him the courage to pursue a full-time career in food. While working with Priscilla Carluccio (he had already done a stint in Antonio's kitchen as pudding and salad chef) he came to the attention of Angela Mason, the formidable food editor of the British *Mail on Sunday*'s mighty *YOU* magazine. Mason, always a champion of new talent, offered him the opportunity to produce an occasional food column. 'Angela saw something in me and wanted to give me a break, which was really nice. To just go straight into a national paper and not have to work my way up as a food stylist and all that kind of thing.' Nice indeed.

His print career included the food editorship of the UK's *Red* magazine and a lengthy stint at *The Sunday Times*. These days he also contributes to the BBC's second food magazine, *Olive*. He has often been exasperated by what he considers to be the British food media's reluctance to take risks. 'We're so staid sometimes, it's almost like we don't understand food unless it's funny and colourful.' (I share his viewpoint; it echoes my own belief in the 'pantomime dame syndrome'; that is, that the British like their food served up with a dash of slapstick, hence the tradition — and success — of TV food celebrities such as Ainsley Harriott and the Two Fat Ladies). 'And it's still like that,' Hendy continues. 'We've got TV chefs like Gordon Ramsay who have to behave in a ridiculous fashion for everyone to watch them.'

He has, at times, had a reputation for being, shall we say, strong-willed, and is rarely afraid to voice his opinions. He claims his refusal to compromise his creative views led him to pick up the camera. 'I couldn't get anybody to do what I wanted, so I thought why don't I just bloody well get on and do it. Take the photographs, do the lot and then I've only got myself to blame.'

Whatever his views on British food media, Hendy understands that eating habits have changed, probably irrevocably. That was the premise upon which he based his book *Home Cook* (Headline, 2004). 'Everyone's working harder,' he explains. 'There's no one at home preparing food all day long. It doesn't work that way anymore. We're all cutting corners and buying stuff ready-prepared or half-prepared so we can chuck it all together for speed.' I found *Home Cook* reassuringly down to earth, living up to its author's claim of being a combination of 'stuff you would cook at home now, stuff your mum made that you still want and stuff we'll be doing in the future'. It's refreshingly less self-conscious than some of his previous work (the recipe for his mum's turkey curry, for instance, calls for tinned mandarin segments).

Travel photography is a recent string to the Hendy bow. He is a passionate traveller. 'Home cook around the world' is how he has neatly described his approach to food and personally, I think it's the milieu that suits him best. Admittedly it's a coffee-table book that is likely to attract only experienced cooks, but anyone who has seen his *Food and Travels: Asia* will know he has a superb eye for capturing the mood of a country through detail, and working it seamlessly with local food. The images are exquisite.

Interestingly, earlier in our conversation, Hendy said that what drew him early in his career to *Vogue Entertaining + Travel* was the way in which the Australian magazine brilliantly fused food and fashion. 'I loved its bravery', he says. It appealed to his stylist's eye. In many respects, his food and travel photo-reportage represents a similar fusion, substituting exotic (but fashionable) real-life destinations for the dining rooms and dinner parties of the past. One particular image, shot in Vietnam, won him the World's Best Food Photographer award at the World Food Media Awards in Adelaide in 2003. He also picked up the World's Best Food Journalist gong at the same awards. 'I was so elated, I'd never won an award before and then I got two, and both gold. I was crying.'

Bearing in mind that a word doesn't exist to describe what he does, and in a publishing world that prefers its talent to have one definable skill, Alastair Hendy the writer-cum-cook-cum-stylist-cum photographer is a puzzle. Not everyone gets him. But I will stick my neck out and say that I have always considered him the most forward-looking food stylist in the UK. He's an innovator, and sometimes people are wary of those. 'I see lines of plates in photographs, that whole Zen thing is still going on,' he wails. 'We should have dropped all that a long time ago but people are still doing it, and folded napkins under plates. I can't bear it. I mean what are they *doing* there?'

'For this "Japan in a bowl", grated radish, extra seaweed, a nip of wasabi and a bottle of Kikkoman should all be at hand as you eat. It's a great get-together of store-cupboard stuff, that with the addition of an easy slice of salmon and a few crunchy leaves is invigoratingly fresh, and my perfect one-bowl supper. Dashi *is a Japanese stock made from dried bonito, handily available in instant sachet form. Bottled teriyaki marinade could be used instead of mirin and soy. I want you to cook this, not run a mile.'*

one-bowl noodles

four 150 g (5 oz) skinned salmon
fillets (wild, if you can)
salt and pepper
60 ml (2 fl oz/¼ cup) mirin
60 ml (2 fl oz/¼ cup) dark soy sauce
400 g (14 oz) soba (buckwheat)
noodles or other wheat noodles
vegetable oil
1.5 litres (52 fl oz/6 cups) Japanese
dashi stock (use an instant sachet)
or light chicken stock
1 tablespoon toasted sesame seeds
1 tablespoon crumbled toasted *nori*
seaweed (the type used to
wrap sushi)
4 spring onions (scallions),
finely shredded
a good handful of young crunchy
leaves, such as watercress
or anything oriental

Rub the fillets with a little salt and pepper, place in a sandwich bag and pour in half of the mirin and half of the soy sauce. Lightly massage it around the fish, then leave for about an hour or however long you've got, turning occasionally.

Meanwhile, cook the noodles according to the packet directions. To perfect your noodles, and this is for perfectionists, add 125 ml (4 fl oz/½ cup) cold water to the pot twice during cooking, allowing the water to come back to the boil after each addition (this arrested cooking technique firms them up). Drain, then rinse under cold water.

Rub the marinated salmon with a little oil and place in a preheated (preferably non-stick) frying pan and sear for about 2 minutes on each side, splashing in a drop of the marinade toward the end — this will bung in teryaki flavour, caramelize it beautifully and keep it deep pink in the middle. No shifting it about now while it's searing.

Bring the soup stock to a hearty bubble with the remaining mirin and soy sauce. Divide the noodles and stock among four generous bowls. Sprinkle each with sesame seeds and crumbled seaweed, and top with the salmon, spring onion and leaves.

Chopsticks drawn, spoons on the mark, let's dig in.

Serves 4

'Many good things go on my toast — fried cod's roe, sliced tomatoes with sea salt, and so on. Wild mushrooms are good, but I'm just as happy with those cheap, bulk-buy closed-cap chaps that turn to heaven in this.

Recipes are not written in stone, so I'm often suggesting variations on the theme, as I do here. I can eat this morning, noon and night. The ultimate "on toast". Like childhood, lived on.'

mushrooms on toast

button mushrooms — they can be button chestnut or the regular tiny white ones, or large flat caps, thickly sliced
butter, for frying and buttering
sea salt and loads of twists from the pepper mill
thick slices of white bread — tin loaf or farm house

Fry the mushrooms in some butter until well browned, but don't lower the heat too much, otherwise they'll release all their delicious juices into the pan. Season with salt and plenty of black pepper.

Toast the bread until golden brown and be generous with the butter — you want it almost pooling. Top the toast with the mushrooms and scrape out any of the remaining juices in the pan on top. Twist over some more pepper and serve straight away.

variations: add roughly chopped marjoram, thyme or some sage leaves to the pan, and then you can go in a garlic direction too, if you like. The meaty flat-cap mushrooms are great with a dollop of horseradish cream on top: beat freshly grated horseradish into crème fraîche with finely chopped shallot, and a dash of wine vinegar and some seasoning.

Serves as many as you like

'I love Morocco. I adore its tagines. It's the dried fruit, meat and vegetable connection that does it. One-pot, slow-cooked food sits well in the British climate. Here's one for winter — and lamb shanks are so handy when it comes to dishing up. Make it up well in advance, for the flavours get happier as they get to know each other, then simply reheat for 30–40 minutes in a moderate oven when ready. Eat with couscous or flat breads, and chuck on some fresh mint.'

walnut and fig braised lamb

4 small lamb shanks or around 1 kg (2 lb 4 oz) boned lamb shoulder, cut into large chunks
2 tablespoons olive oil, plus extra for brushing
salt and black pepper
2 large onions, each sliced into 4 thick discs and peeled
1 teaspoon each ground ginger, cinnamon, coriander and cumin
3 sticks cassia bark or cinnamon
4 strips orange zest
500 ml (17 fl oz/2 cups) lamb stock or water, or as needed
10 semi-dried figs
12 walnut halves

Brown the lamb all over in a wide casserole pan in the oil, adding salt and pepper. Remove from the heat, take the lamb out of the pot, place the onion slices across the bottom of the pan, then pop the meat back on top.

Next, sprinkle all the spices over everything, and tuck the pieces of orange zest and the cinnamon around the lamb. Pour in about 500 ml (17 fl oz/2 cups) stock or water — enough to allow the meat to sit in a shallow puddle.

Season again. Cover, bring to a bubble on the hob, then place the pot in a 180° C (350° F/Gas 4) oven (a tad less if using a convection oven) and leave it to murmur away for a good 3 hours.

Halfway through, check on the liquid level, adding the figs and walnuts during the final hour. The meat should be at falling point from the bone, and unctuous. Eat with couscous or flat breads.

Serves 4

203

'The usual scenario is "Quick, I need a little something instant yet home made, stylish and so totally gorgeous everyone will talk about it for days". This is a big tray of a tart that slices into easy squares. No matter how last-minute I am, it's always a beautiful thing. The apricots ooze a delicious concentrate which works wonders with the pastry. If you can't find apricots, use plums instead.

emergency apricot tart

1 kg (2 lb 4 oz) apricots
1 packet ready-made pre-rolled puff pastry
1¹/₂ tablespoons ground almonds or plain (all-purpose) flour
3 tablespoons caster (superfine) sugar
1 egg, lightly beaten
4 tablespoons apricot jam
crème fraîche or thick (double/heavy) cream (or if me, both)

Preheat the oven to 220° C (425° F/Gas 7) — or for convection ovens, nearer 200° C (400° F/Gas 6).

Using a small stubby knife and holding an apricot in the other hand, slice the fruit lengthways into three wedges, allowing the tip of the knife to follow the stone. This is very easy, and your pace will quicken as you master this Jack-the-Ripper action.

Next, unroll the pastry onto a greased baking tray, something near the width of the pastry (and one with a small lip would be ideal). Scatter with the ground almonds or flour and half of the sugar, leaving a border around the edge.

Then line the apricot wedges across the tart, each row overlapping the last, so that the pointy bits stick up a little, and again leaving a small border all around the edge.

Next, scatter over the rest of the sugar, liberally brush all the exposed edges of pastry with the beaten egg and bake on the middle shelf of the oven for about 30 minutes, or until crisped around the edges. The apricots' tips should be lightly seared and the pastry cooked through underneath.

Stir the apricot jam with 2 tablespoons water in a small saucepan over low heat until blended and syrupy, then brush this all over the tart once it has cooled for a few minutes. Eat while freshly baked, with a flood of cream.

Serves 8

At Ballymaloe House I tasted my first oyster and my first sea urchin. The oysters I fell dizzyingly in love with, and I felt absurdly foolish that I'd left it so late to try them. The sea urchin I instantly regretted. At Ballymaloe Cookery School I stood fascinated, in the fine Irish mizzle, while a busload of ladies in headscarves and raincoats scoured the grounds, with the pious intent of pilgrims at Lourdes, for a glimpse of Darina Allen. I have watched the day's catch unloaded at the small fishing harbour of Ballycotton and downed a pint or two of creamy Guinness in the local pub. I have dined with the Allen family and savoured the delicate concentration of flavours in local grilled cod with wild watercress butter, scallion champ and feathery light carrageen, the sweet mousse made with Irish moss — seaweed — from this south-western coast of Ireland. Ballymaloe is a magic place and memories come thick and fast: the crack and spit of a log fire, the delicious pungency of woodsmoke, the chill of a county Cork night. Oatmeal porridge with cream, fresh-baked soda bread and kippers — the glorious, gluttonous pleasures of a Ballymaloe breakfast.

darina allen

But on a crisp autumn morning in 2004, Darina Allen is despondent. The founder of the world-renowned Ballymaloe Cookery School, Allen is the passionately outspoken, crusading doyenne of Irish food, or perhaps more accurately co-doyenne, sharing that honour with her mother-in-law, the redoubtable Myrtle Allen, of neighbouring Ballymaloe House. For more than thirty years, both Allens have stood for good, honest, traditional Irish cooking, in tune with the seasons and the landscape. And in more recent years, Darina Allen has been a high-profile ambassador for the organic movement in Ireland, a champion of artisanal food producers and an enthusiastic advocate of the local farmers' markets that now proliferate in the republic.

On this particular morning, however, she is despairing, convinced that half the population of Ireland must be in a permanent state of indigestion. At the village shop in nearby Shanagarry she counted eleven indigestion remedies on the shelf. 'They wouldn't have the stuff if there wasn't a demand for it. If only you could get people to realize — to just stop and think — that the reason they're feeling so bloody awful is because of whatever they shovelled into themselves today.'

'If you put dirty petrol in the car it'll chug and spatter, it won't go. People don't seem to understand that if they get a lump or a bump or a rash it's very often connected to the food they're eating. We have to encourage people to put more effort into sourcing really good-quality produce. It doesn't have to be expensive, just fresh, local, naturally produced food in season. If they put that on the table they won't have to spend quite so much at the chemist.'

Allen is the eldest of nine children and grew up in a household 'where you absolutely had three meals a day. It was lovely, simple, family food, though with nine children, by the time you'd cleared up one meal it was nearly time to start another.' While studying at hotel school in Dublin in the late 1960s, she realised cooking was the thing she enjoyed most.

'I wanted to know how to make ice cream, pâtés, terrines and soufflés. And I wanted to know about fresh herbs. We had parsley, thyme and chives at home but what was basil? What were marjoram, tarragon and lemon grass? At that time you could count the number of good restaurants in Ireland on one hand and maybe even have a finger or two left over, and none of those would take a woman in the kitchen. Men were chefs, women ran tea shops.'

One of Allen's tutors told her about a farmer's wife down near Cork who had opened a restaurant in her own home. 'She said, "I think it's miles from the road, but don't you come from the country? It's probably all right for you".' The farmer's wife, of course, was Myrtle Allen, who would have doubtless seen more than a little of herself in the young woman who travelled down from Dublin for a job.

'So I came to Ballymaloe,' continues Allen, 'and I met this grey-haired woman who taught me the opposite of all I'd learned. I was like a sponge, soaking up everything she said. Not everyone can say this about their mother-in-law, but she's truly inspirational and a visionary. She was convinced that if she fed her family a healthy diet, they had a fairly good chance of being healthy. That was her primary motivation, that and the fact that my father-in-law loved his food.' In an era when chicken Maryland and scampi vied for supremacy on

sophisticated menus, Myrtle Allen was serving fresh mackerel from Ballycotton, rice pudding, swedes, turnips and parsnips. 'All sorts of food you never saw on restaurant menus then. Myrtle cooked the food she served to her family and her friends and the customers loved it.'

Within a few months of joining Myrtle at Ballymaloe House, Darina met the Allens' eldest son, Tim. The couple married in 1970 and the cookery school was opened in 1983. Ballymaloe's off-beat — for the time — philosophy of organic, seasonal cooking eventually attracted students from all over the world ('we just used the food of our farm and our area and it seemed the logical thing to do') and Darina Allen's profile grew apace with that of the school.

Over the twenty or more years since the first students stood at the Ballymaloe stoves, Allen has written numerous cookbooks, penned regular magazine and newspaper articles (she still has a weekly column in the *Irish Examiner*) and has made eight or nine television series (even she can't remember how many) for Ireland's RTE network. She is an Irish institution and it's small wonder that the good ladies of Cork and beyond seek her photograph, her autograph and her wisdom on the bus tours to the Ballymaloe Cookery School. Even a scandal that rocked the Allen family (and indeed, the whole of Ireland) a few years ago doesn't appear to have diminished her standing.

And rightly so. Allen, and a small band of cohorts across the world (which include her 'soul sister' Alice Waters in California, Australia's Stephanie Alexander, the Slow Food Movement's Carlo Petrini and the Indian food writer and activist Vandana Shiva) are a strong and necessary force for good. Allen's evangelism — if it can be called that — is not self-serving.

She believes wholeheartedly in the role good nutrition could play in the world's growing health crisis and is not afraid to voice her opinions. She is involved with the Food Safety Authority of Ireland, the Irish Food Board, the Irish Organic Trust, and increasingly, the Slow Food movement. 'I am very concerned about what we are passing on to coming generations in the way of genes,' she told me. 'There are all kind of indications that things have gone seriously wrong and those of us who are aware have a duty to speak out.'

New students who arrive at Ballymaloe for the school's twelve-week course get an immediate flavour of the Allen Way. 'I know it sounds like aged hippy stuff,' she laughs, 'but the first recipe the students get is how to make compost. I need to shock them into thinking about how their food is produced and where it comes from.'

Allen's despair with the state of Ireland's diet lightens as she discusses a new television idea she would like to get off the ground, a series designed to get people back in the kitchen cooking traditional foods, relearning skills that were once passed down through the generations. 'I want people to sit down around the kitchen table again. It doesn't matter if it's only an omelette or a simple bean stew. Get the damned television out of the kitchen, sit down and share the food together. Bring the pot to the table. It really can be done. We can always make time in life for the things that are important, it's just a question of priorities.'

'Colcannon is one of Ireland's best-loved traditional potato dishes — fluffy mashed potato flecked with cooked cabbage or kale. This recipe uses identical ingredients to make a delicious soup.'

irish colcannon soup

80 g (2³/₄ oz) butter
425 g (15 oz) peeled diced potatoes
110 g (4 oz/³/₄ cup) diced onions
salt and freshly ground pepper
1.1 litres (38 fl oz/4¹/₂ cups) home-made chicken or vegetable stock
450 g (1 lb) savoy cabbage
125 ml (4 fl oz/¹/₂ cup) creamy milk, or as needed

Melt 55 g (2 oz) of the butter in a heavy-bottomed saucepan. When it foams, add the potato and onion and toss them in the butter until well coated. Season with salt and freshly ground pepper. Cover and sweat on a gentle heat for 6–10 minutes. Add the stock, increase the heat and cook until the vegetables are soft but not coloured.

Meanwhile, make the buttered cabbage. Remove and discard the tough outer leaves from the cabbage. Divide into four, cut out the stalks and then cut into fine shreds across the grain. Put 2–3 table-spoons of water in a wide saucepan with the remaining butter and a pinch of salt. Bring to the boil, add the cabbage and toss constantly over a high heat, then cover for a few minutes. Toss again and add some more salt, freshly ground pepper and an extra knob of butter.

Purée in a blender or food processor, then add the cabbage to the soup (or purée the cabbage with the soup if you prefer a smoother texture). Taste and adjust the seasoning. Thin with creamy milk to the required consistency.

Serves 6

'Yeast is a living organism that needs warmth, moisture and nourishment to grow. Have the ingredients and equipment at blood heat. White or brown sugar, honey, golden syrup, treacle or molasses may be used. Each will give the bread a slightly different flavour. At Ballymaloe, we use treacle and a stone-ground wholemeal flour. The amount of natural moisture in the flour varies according to atmospheric conditions. The quantity of water should be altered accordingly. The dough should be just too wet to knead — in fact, it does not require kneading. I give two quantities according to whether you want to make one loaf or several.

Dried yeast may be used instead of baker's yeast. Follow the same method but use half the weight given for fresh yeast, and allow longer to rise. Fast-acting yeast may also be used; follow the instructions on the packet.'

ballymaloe brown yeast bread

to make one 13 x 20 cm (5 x 8 inch) loaf
450 g (1 lb) wholemeal (whole-wheat) flour or 400 g (14 oz) wholemeal flour plus 50 g (1³/₄ oz) strong white flour
1 teaspoon salt
1 teaspoon black treacle
425 ml (15 fl oz) water, at blood heat
25 g (1 oz) fresh, non-GM yeast
sunflower oil
sesame seeds, optional

to make four or five 13 x 20 cm (5 x 8 inch) loaves
1.8 kg (4 lb) wholemeal (whole-wheat) flour or 1.5 kg (3 lb 5 oz) wholemeal flour plus 225 g (8 oz) strong white flour
1 tablespoon salt
2–3 well-rounded teaspoons black treacle
1.6–1.7 litres (56–59 fl oz) water, at blood heat
50–100g (1³/₄–3¹/₂ oz) fresh, non-GM yeast
sunflower oil
sesame seeds, optional

Preheat the oven to 230° C (450° F/Gas 8).

Mix the flour with the salt. The ingredients should all be at room temperature. In a small bowl or heatproof jug, mix the treacle with some of the water (about 140 ml/4¹/₂ fl oz) for 1 loaf and 290 ml/10 fl oz for 4–5 loaves) and crumble in the yeast.

Sit the bowl for a few minutes in a warm place to allow the yeast to start to work. Grease the bread tin(s) with sunflower oil. Meanwhile, check to see if the yeast is rising. After 4–5 minutes it will have a creamy and slightly frothy appearance on top.

When ready, stir and pour the yeast mixture and all the remaining water into the flour to make a loose, wet dough. The mixture should be too wet to knead. Put the mixture into the greased tins. Sprinkle the top of the loaves with sesame seeds if you like. Put the tins in a warm place somewhere close to the cooker, or near a radiator perhaps. Cover the tins with a tea towel to prevent a skin from forming. Just as the head comes to the top of the tin, remove the tea towel and pop the loaves in the oven for 50–60 minutes, or until they look nicely browned and sound hollow when tapped. They will rise a little further in the oven. This is called oven spring. If, however, the bread rises to the top of the tin before it goes into the oven it will continue to rise and flow over the edges.

We usually remove the loaves from the tins about 10 minutes before the end of cooking and put them back into the oven to crisp all round, but if you like a softer crust there's no need to do this.

Above: irish colcannon soup
Opposite: baked plaice or dover sole with herb butter

'This is a very simple "master recipe" that can be used not only for plaice and sole but for any very fresh flat fish, including brill, turbot, dabs, flounder and lemon sole. Depending on the size of the fish, it can be a starter or a main course. It's also delicious with hollandaise sauce, mousseline or beurre blanc.'

baked plaice or dover sole with herb butter

4 very fresh whole plaice (flounder) or sole
salt and freshly ground pepper

herb butter
85 g (3 oz/¹/₃ cup) butter
4 teaspoons mixed finely chopped fresh parsley, chives, fennel and thyme leaves

Preheat the oven to 190° C (375° F/Gas 5).

Turn each fish on its side and remove the head. Wash the fish and clean the slit very thoroughly. With a sharp knife, cut through the skin right round the fish, just where the 'fringe' meets the flesh. Be careful to cut neatly and to cross the side cuts at the tail or it will be difficult to remove the skin later on.

Sprinkle the fish with salt and pepper and lay them in 7 mm (¹/₃ inch) of water in a shallow baking tin. Bake for 20–30 minutes, according to the size of the fish. The water should have just evaporated as the fish is cooked. Check to see whether the fish is cooked by lifting the flesh from the bone at the head; it should lift off the bone easily and be quite white with no trace of pink.

Meanwhile, melt the butter and stir in the freshly chopped herbs. Just before serving, catch the skin down near the tail and pull it off gently (the skin will tear badly if not properly cut). Lift the fish onto hot plates and spoon the herb butter over them. Serve immediately.

Serves 4

'When I'm driving through country lanes in late May or early June, suddenly I spy the elderflower coming into bloom. Then I know it's time to go and search on gooseberry bushes for the hard, green fruit, far too under-ripe at that stage to eat raw, but wonderful cooked in tarts or fools or in this delicious compote.

Elderflowers have an extraordinary affinity with green gooseberries and by a happy arrangement of nature they are both in season at the same time.'

green gooseberry and elderflower compote

900 g (2 lb) green gooseberries
2 or 3 elderflower heads
600 ml (21 fl oz)
450 g (1 lb) sugar
fresh elderflowers, to decorate

Top and tail the gooseberries.

Tie the elderflower heads in a little square of muslin, put in a stainless steel or enamelled saucepan, add the sugar and cover with 600 ml (21 fl oz) cold water. Bring slowly to the boil and continue to boil for 2 minutes. Add the gooseberries and simmer just until the fruit bursts. Allow to cool. Serve in a pretty bowl and decorate with fresh elderflowers.

Serves 6–8

variation: green gooseberry and elderflower fool
Liquidize the compote and mix with softly whipped cream to taste (about half the volume of whipped cream to fruit purée). Serve chilled with shortbread biscuits.

martin boetz

Sydney can be a fickle place at the best of times, but especially when it comes to restaurants. This week's hotspot? Next week's cliché. Perhaps it's the same the world over, but because Sydney embraces its food with such passion, the acclaim seems louder, and the failure — if and when it comes — more painful and more public. It's a tough (or an exceptionally good) establishment that stays the course, and a truly remarkable one that becomes a legend.

When I arrived in Sydney late in 1999, a new Thai restaurant called Longrain in the inner-city suburb of Surry Hills was creating ripples of excitement. In a city that brims over with Thai food, Longrain had a smart formula. Take the city's favourite cuisine and combine it with an equal passion for the new, glamorous and sexy. Add a cutting-edge interior, an anarchic location (Surry Hills was just emerging as an alternative cultural nucleus, like London's Hoxton or New York's meatpacking district) and the integrity of a young, highly creative chef with an impressive cv: Martin Boetz. No wonder those fickle Sydneysiders queued for hours (and still do) for Longrain's exquisite betel-wrapped ocean trout, rich caramelized pork hock and the dish that quickly became Boetz's signature, delicate egg 'nets' stuffed with pork, prawn and abundant fresh herbs.

Frankfurt-born Boetz (it's pronounced 'berts' although most people default to 'boats') is a one-off. A German-born Australian with a Brisbane accent who adores Italy and cooks sublime Thai food. Along with his quietly-spoken business partner, Sam Christie, who discreetly manages the controlled chaos of the Longrain floor, Boetz has been the public face of the restaurant since it opened on 27 August 1999. He still works the open-plan stoves at least four nights each week, orchestrating his team of enthusiastic young chefs. 'Longrain set the tone for modern Asian restaurants in Sydney, it raised the bar,' he says. 'It all just works somehow, it just happens.'

In August 2000, exactly a year after opening, the *Sydney Morning Herald*'s *Good Food Guide* (edited by Jill Dupleix and Terry Durack) awarded Longrain two highly coveted chef's hats, the local equivalent of Michelin stars. 'Martin Boetz cooks the freshest, classiest Thai food in Sydney,' proclaimed the anonymous reviewer, 'and his menu is one of those rarities where nearly every dish is a favourite.' Always maintaining a steady

16/20 (which has variously stood for 'lovely', 'really lovely' and 'a bit of *wow* factor' on the *Good Food Guide*'s curiously erratic scale), Longrain's 2003 entry mentioned the now famous caipiroskas, the vodka-based 'stick drinks' (in bar parlance) that became the most imitated cocktail in Sydney. By 2004 and still hanging on to those two hats, the guide had coined the phrase 'Mod Thai' to contain Boetz's occasional dabblings into Chinese flavours, while the 2005 guide paid the restaurant a back-handed compliment with a pot shot at Longrain's infamous queues. 'Good things do come,' wrote the reviewer, 'to those who wait, and wait, and wait.'

Boetz learnt his craft from the Thai master, Sydney chef David Thompson. 'He tortured me', he laughs, recalling his early days as an apprentice in Thompson's Darley Street Thai kitchen. 'Well, he worked me quite hard, anyway. He must have seen something in me. But it was pretty intense work.' Thompson must certainly have seen a talent in the young apprentice. After a ten-month break in Italy — 'which really refined and improved my cooking skills' — and still only in his mid-20s, Boetz was offered the position of head chef at Thompson's Sailors Thai restaurant in the Rocks district of Sydney.

The only time Martin Boetz ever cooked for me at home, he cooked Italian food, expertly. Of course he wasn't going to create the stir-fries or curries that he cooks each night of the week (amazing that he wanted to cook at all), but his passion for Italian food is interesting. For a young chef (he is now 36) generally credited with being Sydney's — and one of Australia's — finest Thai cooks, he can seem oddly blasé about his craft. Almost as if his skill, and the success it has brought, has taken him by surprise.

'I love the generosity of Italian food culture and the flavours of rustic Italian food. I see a lot of similarities between Thai and Italian food. People live for the next meal and talk about food constantly. But I love the flavours of Thai food and I'm into the culture of sharing. Food brings people together. I love the concept of sharing even though it can sometimes be confronting.'

Generosity is a word Boetz uses frequently. He believes the generosity of Longrain's food is key to its success. And later on in our conversation, he names Australian cook and food writer Maggie Beer as an unusual mentor for a Thai chef. 'I love her generosity', he says.

Lunch or dinner in the cavernous Longrain dining room with its wide refectory tables is not for the faint of heart. The noise level can be cacophonous, elbows and shoulders are frequently rubbed and it sometimes feels as if it might be easier to call or text dining companions than shout at them across the expanse of dining table. But the reward is always the sublime food, traditional Thai recipes deftly prepared and adapted to complement fresh Australian produce. Darkly aromatic chicken, spiced with cassia bark, star anise and Sichuan pepper, is enhanced by Boetz's insistence on free-range Barossa chicken from South Australia, while many of the dishes call for the Australian seafood that the chef loves — perch, mud crab, kingfish and prawns.

Chefs' hats in the *Good Food Guide* are important for sure, but for Boetz personally, the invitation in 2003 to cook for the then Indonesian president Megawati Sukarnoputri at her home in Jakarta was a tribute to his skills. 'An Indonesian couple that live between Jakarta and Sydney regularly frequent Longrain,' he explains, 'and I was their gift to her! They asked me if I would go over and cook.'

'I cooked for 60 that night. We prepped in a hotel and then cooked at the house — in the garage — in 35 degrees of heat. Luckily I had a clean jacket to whack on and meet Megawati. I spoke to her in Indonesian, I'd rehearsed the whole thing!'

All that Boetz took from Sydney were curry pastes. Relying on his instinct for fresh local produce, he created a menu for the presidential banquet of duck and winter melon soup with shiitake mushrooms, a yellow curry of river prawns and spiced duck with plum sauce. He agrees it was an honour to be invited and he's proud of what he achieved that night, but would he ever do it again? There's not a split second of consideration. 'No.'

It's a measure of Longrain's success that the vexed question of whether a Melbourne version would open kept Sydney food journalists guessing for years. At the time of writing (early in 2005) Boetz is packing his bags for a spell in the chillier city. Longrain Melbourne is finally scheduled to open in the city's smart Little Bourke Street and he will of course preside over everything. He knows Melbourne will present a challenge. The city doesn't enjoy Sydney's traditional affinity with Asian cooking and Melburnian hearts and minds are maybe harder won. 'There's a significant difference between what Sydney and Melbourne people want to eat,' admits Boetz, 'and there's a big difference between what restaurants serve in each city, not to mention the availability of produce.'

It strikes me that, given Boetz's skills, his love of Italian food and the Melburnian predilection for all things Mediterranean, an Italian Longrain — called Arborio naturally — might be just the job down south. But instead, I ask Boetz about the long-term future. 'At the moment my ambition is simply to open another Longrain and run two restaurants very well. After that, maybe something overseas.' He's keen to spend some time in Germany (he left when he was four years old) and thinks the Longrain concept would be 'amazing' there, perhaps in Berlin. His first cookbook, *Longrain: Modern Thai Food* (Hardie Grant) was published in 2003 and demonstrates the inseparability of the Boetz and Longrain names. I ask if Longrain could survive without him. Not a moment's hesitation. 'No,' he says, with sudden Teutonic solemnity, before breaking into that big, gap-toothed Australian smile.

'The crispness of the pork is incredible against the soft texture of the cuttlefish. It's a traditional Thai combination, although squid is more usual. I prefer cuttlefish as it's more tender. This dish has been a regular on the Longrain menu since we started.'

crisp salted pork and cuttlefish salad

200 g (7 oz) belly pork
50 g (1³/₄ oz) sea salt
100 ml (3¹/₂ fl oz) rice vinegar
1 litre (35 fl oz/4 cups) vegetable oil
150 g (5¹/₂ oz) cuttlefish, cleaned
and scored on the underside
thick sweet soy sauce, optional
4 spring onions (scallions),
shredded
2 red chillies, julienned
1 x 4 cm (1¹/₂ inch) piece ginger,
peeled and julienned
1 bunch each mint and coriander
(cilantro), washed and chopped
3 green bird's eye chillies, finely sliced
1 red shallot, peeled and finely sliced
1 stem Chinese celery, finely sliced
juice of 1 lime

yellow bean soy dressing (makes 3 cups)
5 cloves garlic, peeled
5 red bird's eye chillies
4 cm (1¹/₂ inch) piece ginger, peeled
1 cup light yellow bean sauce
1 cup thick sweet soy sauce
250 ml (9 fl oz/1 cup) rice vinegar
¹/₂ cup thick yellow bean sauce
230 g (8 oz/1 cup) caster (superfine)
sugar

Set a steamer over boiling water and steam the pork, covered, for 35 minutes until cooked. Cool slightly, then prick the skin all over with a fork and massage the salt and vinegar into the skin. Rub a little salt and vinegar on the other side as well. Place the pork on a cake rack with a tray underneath to catch any drips as the pork cools. When cool, remove the pork from the rack and refrigerate for 1–2 hours until it firms (this makes the pork easier to slice).

Slice the pork into long, fine strips along the grain.

Heat the oil in a wok until just smoking and fry the pork until brown and crisp, 3–4 minutes. Drain on paper towel and set aside.

Bring a pot of water to the boil, add salt to season and blanch the cuttlefish. Once it curls up, it's done. Refresh in cold water and set aside. You can grill the cuttlefish instead of blanching if you like — rub with some thick sweet soy sauce first before grilling.

Mix the rest of the ingredients together in a bowl. Toss the crisp pork and cuttlefish with the salad and 150 ml (5 fl oz) of the dressing and place on a serving plate.

For the dressing, using a mortar and pestle, pound the garlic, chillies and ginger to a uniform paste. Put the paste and the rest of the dressing ingredients in a heavy-based pan, bring to the boil and simmer for 5 minutes. Cool and store in a clip-top jar.

Serves 4 as part of a shared meal

martin boetz

'This dates back to my Darley Street Thai days and has been a favourite at Longrain since the day we opened. The braised beef is from a traditional Chinese recipe, while the hot and sour salad is the Thai influence. The richness of the meaty braising liquid will be balanced by the hot-and-sour dressing in the salad, giving a good balance of flavours.'

braised beef shin with a hot and sour salad

braised beef
one 200 g (7 oz) piece beef shin
1 tablespoon thick sweet soy sauce
100 ml (3½ fl oz) vegetable oil
5 cloves garlic, peeled
4 cm (1½ inch) piece ginger, peeled
1 coriander (cilantro) root, scraped and cleaned
1 small red onion
100 ml (3½ fl oz) Chinese rice wine
50 g (1¾ oz) rock candy, crushed
50 ml (1½ fl oz) oyster sauce
500 ml (17 fl oz/2 cups) chicken stock
50 ml (1½ fl oz) Chinese black vinegar
1 teaspoon sea salt

hot & sour salad
50 ml (1½ fl oz) lime juice
½ teaspoon red chilli powder
1 tablespoon fish sauce
2 green bird's eye chillies, finely sliced
10 coriander (cilantro) leaves
10 mint leaves
1 spring onion (scallion), finely shredded
1 red Asian shallot, peeled and finely sliced
½ large red chilli, seeded and finely sliced

To make the braised beef, rub the thick sweet soy sauce all over the beef. Heat a little vegetable oil in a pan and seal the beef on all sides. Place in a deep braising pan.

Pound the garlic, ginger, coriander root and onion to a paste. Heat some oil in a heavy-based saucepan and fry the pounded ingredients until golden brown. Discard the excess oil and deglaze with the Chinese rice wine. Add the rock candy, oyster sauce and chicken stock. Bring to the boil and skim off all the scum. Pour the liquid over the beef. Cover with baking (parchment) paper and foil, and braise on top of the stove for 1½ hours until the meat is soft.

Remove the meat and set aside. Strain the liquid and boil hard to reduce by a third. Add the vinegar and salt and taste — the mixture should taste rich and meaty.

To make the hot and sour salad, combine the lime juice, chilli powder, fish sauce and chillies. This dressing should taste very hot and sour. In a stainless steel bowl, toss together the rest of the salad ingredients and add the dressing.

To serve, cut the braised beef into 1 cm (⅓ inch) slices and reheat in the reduced braising liquid. Place the sliced beef in the middle of the serving bowl, and pour over a generous amount of the braising liquid. Place the hot and sour salad on top of the beef, and pour some of the dressing into the meaty juices. Serve with steamed rice.

Serves 6–8 a part of a shared meal

martin boetz

green curry of prawns

green curry paste (makes 1½ cups)
1 medium-sized red onion, chopped
5 cloves garlic, peeled
4 cm (1½ inch) piece galangal, peeled
2 stems lemon grass, white part only
½ teaspoon sea salt
6 coriander (cilantro) roots, scraped and cleaned
6 long green chillies, seeded
8 green bird's eye chillies
2 tablespoons wild ginger
2.5 cm (1 inch) piece fresh turmeric
1 tablespoon roasted shrimp paste
1 tablespoon grated kaffir lime zest

spice mix
1½ tablespoons coriander seeds
1 tablespoon cumin seeds
1 tablespoon mace
1 teaspoon white peppercorns
1 tablespoon sea salt
150 ml (5 fl oz) fresh coconut cream
or 100 ml (3½ fl oz) vegetable oil
3 tablespoons green curry paste (above)
4 fresh kaffir lime leaves
6 pea eggplants
100 ml (3½ fl oz) Thai fish sauce
100 g (3½ oz) palm sugar, shaved
300 ml (10½ fl oz) coconut milk
1 apple eggplant, sliced
2 long green chillies, seeded and sliced
50 g (1¾ oz) fresh bamboo shoots, sliced
3 baby corn, halved
6 raw large king prawns (jumbo shrimp), body shell removed, deveined, head and tails left intact
½ cup Thai basil leaves

To make the paste, using a mortar and pestle, pound the onion, garlic, galangal, lemon grass and the salt to a uniform paste. Remove from the mortar and place in a food processor.

Add to the mortar the coriander roots, chillies, ginger, turmeric, shrimp paste and lime zest. Pound this to a uniform paste, then add to food processor and blend everything to a smooth paste. It should have a good green colour with a hint of fluoro coming from the turmeric.

To make the spice mix, wet the coriander, cumin and mace, drain and dry-roast with the peppercorns and salt in a small heavy-based pan or wok over a medium heat for 10–15 minutes. This will give all the spices ample time to roast all the way through, and do roast slowly for that length of time as they need to be very fragrant when done. Pound, using a mortar and pestle, then grind in small batches in a spice mill or coffee grinder to a fine powder. Pass through a fine mesh sieve. Stir the spices into the paste, mix well and place in an airtight container.

Heat a heavy-based pan and add the coconut cream or vegetable oil. If using the coconut cream, keep cooking and stirring until it splits before you add 3 tablespoons of the curry paste. If using the oil, fry the paste until fragrant and the oil is released. (The remainder of the paste will keep in the refrigerator for 4–6 days, or you can freeze it.)

Add the lime leaves and pea eggplants and stir into the paste. Add the fish sauce and palm sugar, moisten with coconut milk and bring to the boil. Taste for seasoning — the mixture should be hot, salty and slightly sweet. Add more seasoning at this point if needed.

Add the apple eggplant, chilli, bamboo shoot, corn and prawns. Reduce the heat to a simmer and continue to cook for 3 minutes. Fold or stir through the basil, remove from the heat and spoon into a serving bowl. Serve with steamed jasmine rice.

Serves 4 as part of a shared meal

martin boetz

'At Longrain we use duck eggs for the custard which make it quite wicked, especially with the richness of the palm sugar. This dish is our take on a traditional Thai dessert in which eggs, palm sugar and coconut cream are mixed together and steamed. It's often served on black sticky rice or even sprinkled with deep-fried shallots. The addition of fresh turmeric in the caramel gives it a golden colour and the pandanus leaf a fresh, grassy taste. Two types of palm sugar are used for the caramel in this dish: black palm sugar is an Indonesian gula jawa; the other is paler and has a less smoky flavour. All are available from Asian foodstores.'

caramel custard with grilled banana

palm sugar caramel (makes 2 cups)
100 ml (3¹/₂ fl oz) water
¹/₂ cup rock candy, crushed
180 g (6¹/₄ oz/1 cup) shaved palm sugar
90 g (3 oz/¹/₂ cup) shaved black palm sugar
3 cm (1¹/₄ inch) piece fresh turmeric, peeled and sliced
1 pandanus leaf

custard
6 duck eggs
500 ml (17 fl oz/2 cups) coconut cream
1 teaspoon sea salt
1¹/₂ cups palm sugar caramel (see above)

6 ripe sugar bananas
3 tablespoons palm sugar caramel (above), extra
coconut cream

To make the palm sugar caramel, combine the water and sugars in a heavy-based pan over a medium heat. Bring to the boil and reduce for 5 minutes. Add the turmeric and pandanus leaf and continue to cook for a further 5 minutes. Take off the heat and allow to cool.

Preheat the oven to 150° C (300° F/Gas 2). Place six 180 ml (6 fl oz) ramekins in a deep baking tin.

To make the custard, combine all the ingredients together in a mixing bowl. Mix well, then strain into a jug with a pouring lip. Pour the custard into the ramekins. To ensure a smooth top on the finished caramel, use a spoon to skim off any bubbles that occur. Add enough hot water to come halfway up the sides of the ramekins. Cover the top of the baking tin with a layer each of baking (parchment) paper and foil to prevent steam or water getting into the custard. Bake for 35–40 minutes. Check after 35 minutes — the custards are ready when they have a firm jelly-like wobble and the tops are set.

Gently squeeze the bananas while still in their peel to soften the flesh. Set a grill (broiler) to a medium-high heat and grill (broil) until the peel blackens, about 3 minutes on each side. Take off the heat and discard the peel.

To serve, place a ramekin on a serving plate and the banana next to it. Drizzle with extra caramel and coconut cream.

Serves 6

There was that man who wouldn't sign The Beatles because he said they'd never catch on. Then there was the one who said rock and roll would be a five-minute wonder. I'm sure there have been other sages who predicted the swift demise of junk food or denim jeans. Their names are irrelevant, what matters is their toe-curling lack of judgement. Well, meet yours truly, The Man Who Turned Down Jamie Oliver.

jamie oliver

'You must meet wiz Jamie', said my good friend, the French (and obviously very intuitive) photographer Jean Cazals. 'Ee will be ze next beeg theeng.' This would have been 1998, I was editing *Food Illustrated* and Oliver was working as a sous-chef at the iconic River Café in Hammersmith, west London. Stardom was crouching in the wings, though; after all, Cazals was already shooting a book with him and no less than five production companies had called Oliver the morning after his walk-on part in a television documentary about the River Café, offering him a series. So just how big does a Next Big Thing have to be before I see it?

Oliver rocked into my world one morning on that scooter, with a crash helmet under his arm and a vocabulary that I swear really did include the odd 'lovely jubbly.' At least that's how I remember it; maybe television persona and memory have fused. We talked over coffee. Oliver had seen *Food Illustrated* and liked what he saw. He wanted a column; I wasn't sure where I could fit him in. How would he sit alongside all our other regulars? I liked his chutzpah but wasn't he a bit young, a little wet behind the ears?

'He's not really us', I reported back to the editorial team when Oliver had scootered off into the wintry London morning. 'Let's put him on the back burner.' That's editor-speak for 'Let's forget about it'. Jamie mate, a right pukka pig's ear I made of that one.

Funnily enough, Jamie Oliver did quite nicely without that *Food Illustrated* column. He's arguably the world's most famous chef, and from the evidence I gathered while writing this book, I'd say that along with the late British food writer Elizabeth David, Oliver has probably done more than anyone to influence the way we all cook in the last fifty years. While the blokey chatter might not be to everyone's taste, nobody can deny the impact he has had on the eating habits of Britain, of Australia, indeed of every country in which his television series are shown and his books sold. The phrase you will hear time and time again is that Oliver has made cooking 'cool', acceptable and desirable, for a food-dysfunctional generation whose idea of a good meal pre-Jamie might have been a takeaway in front of the television or computer screen. Terence Conran, who has done a thing or two himself to put British food on the map, says Oliver 'has done more for getting young people interested in food than anybody else. I have stepsons in their early twenties who cook, and why do they cook? Because Jamie Oliver has inspired them, not their mother and certainly not their stepfather!'

The second time I met Oliver was in 2001, in Melbourne, a few months before the launch of *ABC delicious.* magazine. He was on a whistlestop tour of Australia and stopped the Collins Street traffic — quite literally — while photographer Mark Roper snapped him for our launch issue. Oliver was tired, jet-lagged, hungry (a crazy schedule of interviews and PAs had overlooked the basics of breakfast, lunch and dinner) and concerned about his wife Jools, pregnant with their first baby back in Britain, but he was the consummate pro.

He gave *ABC delicious.*, a magazine that had not even launched, an exclusive interview, and when I watched him perform at Melbourne's Good Food Show a day or so later, I realised that Oliver was a unique talent. He had the looks, the wit, the precision timing and the easy command of everyone in that thousand-seat theatre. He had what TV moguls would define as the X factor. And incidentally, he could cook quite brilliantly.

In Britain, Oliver has rarely been out of the public eye, whether it be his marriage to Jools, the birth of daughters Poppy and Daisy, his shelf of best-selling cookbooks, his much-hyped friendship with the then Pitt-Anistons or the sheer brilliance of his Fifteen Foundation, which, under Oliver's guidance, mentors disadvantaged young people to train as chefs. The resulting television documentary, *Jamie's Kitchen*, culminated with the opening of his restaurant Fifteen in north London. His recent scheme to improve the quality of school dinners (which won him a Glenfiddich Award for his contribution to the understanding and appreciation of food in the UK) has struck a similar chord with the British public.

In October 2001 Oliver was back in Australia, this time in Sydney, and as editor of *ABC delicious.* I was invited by department store David Jones to interview him in front of almost a thousand shoppers. What sounded to me like a terrifying ordeal was in reality a pleasure, with a rapt audience hanging on Oliver's every word, before queuing up in their hundreds to buy his latest book. Oliver has maintained his strong links with *ABC delicious.* in Australia and with its sister edition in Britain, and I hope both magazines have done him proud. He certainly deserves it. Just as he did that morning in 1998 when The Man Who Turned Down Jamie Oliver put him on the back burner.

When I travelled to Britain from Australia to research *The Accidental Foodie* in October 2004, Jamie Oliver was away on location. Our schedules refused to coincide but he was reluctant to let me down. Instead, we agreed to talk via email, from opposite sides of the world, and I have decided to reproduce the conversation in its entirety.

NW: Jamie, when you look back, can you believe the level of success you have achieved in such a short space of time?

JO: No, I can't really. It's been a roller coaster ride ever since I was 21.

What are you most proud of?

My marriage, my kids, my friends and my students. My first book was like having a baby and felt like a real achievement back then. It was amazing!

You have been hugely influential in getting people back in the kitchen. Why do you think that is?

All I've been doing is demystifying the world of the chef. We all eat bacon sarnies too!

Who are your present food heroes and why?

Rose Gray [of London's River Café] is probably one of my biggest influences. She's an incredible lady and was totally inspirational. All my other food heroes are the suppliers I work with. Also, my students inspire me. I find that when you teach them the basics, you end up teaching yourself again. And Gennaro Contaldo. He is my Italian food mentor, and my second dad in London. He runs the most beautiful restaurant in Charlotte Street called Passione, which I eat at whenever I can.

Why do you think the River Café continues to be so hugely influential and how important to you was the time you spent there?

My time there was so important. It's run by two women who haven't been trained but both of whom have wonderful palates. They don't give a stuff about trends, all they're interested in is what's great and in season. I still think it's one of the most important restaurants in London.

How do you think food has changed in Britain in the last ten years?

Farmers' markets and smallholders have found support locally. People that care about food are hunting down the good stuff but sadly people who don't care are eating worse than ever.

You are a fan of Australia and have a huge following here. What is it you like about this country?

Australia immediately understood where I was coming from. I think that because of the lifestyle, the weather and the sense of humour, me and my food fitted in like an old friend.

Australia has been acknowledged as a centre of food excellence. Do you look to what's happening here at all for inspiration?

I look everywhere for inspiration. I suppose my immediate foundation is French and Mediterranean cooking and as a result I'm more focused on those. But I find Asian cooking really interesting and exciting.

Can you imagine living anywhere other than Britain?

Yes, by the sea in Italy!

So, describe Jamie Oliver's food.

It's all about stripping food back to the bare essentials, making the most of fresh, seasonal ingredients and encouraging people who've never cooked, or want to learn more about cooking, to have a go.

Do you believe in food trends? Where do you think we're heading?

I think food trends were more noticeable before because we hadn't sorted out refrigerated travel. So when things like sun-dried tomatoes arrived, they were immediately embraced. The world's a really small place now but I'd like to see more Arabic, Persian and southern Indian influences.

What depresses you about current food culture?

The fact that schools think physics is more important than teaching kids how to cook.

On stage, Jamie, you are the ultimate entertainer. Do you enjoy it up there?

I just try to make sure that people are having a laugh. Sometimes I might go a bit OTT, but it's all just good fun.

Do you ever give yourself time to sit back, relax and smell the roses?

Only recently, at the weekend, with my wife Jools and the bambinos.

What would Jamie Oliver's last supper be?

My mum's roast on a Sunday.

229

jamie oliver

'This is one of the best fish pies I've ever made I reckon, and it's incredibly quick to do. I've heard so many anecdotes about fish pie, but one argument I always get told about is the with-or-without-eggs one. People are so passionate about whether to put them in or leave them out, it always gets them going. I love it with the eggs, but whatever you do, it'll taste really really good.'

fantastic fish pie

5 large potatoes, peeled and diced into 2.5 cm (1 inch) squares
2 free-range eggs
2 large handfuls of fresh spinach
1 onion, finely chopped
1 carrot, halved and finely chopped
extra virgin olive oil
about 290 ml (10 fl oz) thick (double/heavy) cream
2 good handfuls of grated mature cheddar or parmesan cheese
juice of 1 lemon
1 heaped teaspoon English mustard
1 large handful of flat-leaf (Italian) parsley, finely chopped
450 g (1 lb) haddock or cod fillet, skin removed, pin-boned and sliced into strips
salt and freshly ground black pepper
ground nutmeg (optional)

Preheat the oven to 230° C (450° F/Gas 8). Put the potatoes into salted boiling water and bring back to the boil for 2 minutes. Carefully add the eggs to the pan and cook for a further 8 minutes until hard-boiled, by which time the potatoes should also be cooked. At the same time, steam the spinach in a colander above the pan. This will only take a minute. When the spinach is done, remove from the colander and gently squeeze any excess moisture away.

Then drain the potatoes in the colander. Remove the eggs, cool under cold water, then peel and quarter them. Place to one side. In a separate pan, slowly fry the onion and carrot in a little olive oil for about 5 minutes, then add the cream and bring just to the boil. Remove from the heat and add the cheese, lemon juice, mustard and parsley. Put the spinach, fish and eggs into an appropriately sized earthenware dish and mix together, pouring over the creamy vegetable sauce.

Drain and mash the cooked potatoes — add a bit of olive oil, salt, pepper and a touch of nutmeg if you like. Spread on top of the fish. Don't bother piping it to make it look pretty — it's a homely, hearty thing. Place in the oven for about 25–30 minutes, until the potatoes are golden.

Serve with some nice peas or greens, not forgetting your baked beans and tomato ketchup. Tacky but tasty and that's what I like.

Serves 6

'I've chosen this because it shows that a salad can be a meal in itself, and that fruit in salads can be unbelievable. Peaches are my favourite for their sweetness, along with the milky mozzarella, salty prosciutto and cool mint. You can't mess with the combination and it looks like heaven!

Try to get hold of buffalo mozzarella — I like to crumble a bit of dried chilli over mine, but I'm a chilli freak and you may not be, so you don't have to! And use any mixed leaves you fancy.

The dressing is for four, but you can keep the rest in a jam jar in the fridge.'

mixed leaf salad with mozzarella, mint, peach and prosciutto

for each person
1 ripe peach
1 ball of mozzarella
a couple of slices of prosciutto or parma ham
any mixed salad leaves
mint leaves, torn

olive oil and lemon juice dressing
2 tablespoons lemon juice
5 tablespoons olive oil
salt and freshly ground black pepper, to taste

Pinch the skin of the peaches and peel from the bottom to the top then quarter them. Rip the mozzarella into small pieces and place on a serving plate with the peaches. Lightly season. Lay a couple of slices of prosciutto over the top.

To make the olive oil and lemon juice dressing, mix all the ingredients together.

Dress your mixed salad leaves and torn-up mint with a little of the olive oil and lemon juice dressing. Throw the leaves on top of the plate.

'This is a superb little cocktail. I've used it in demo shows to get the audience going. I'd ask if anyone thought they were boring, and if they stuck up their hand, I'd run out and give them one of these. I would then put another one I'd made down on the stage away from the seating. The challenge was that each person had to finish the first drink and then crawl over to get the second one on the stage, otherwise they would still be boring! Every person I chose was game enough to do it, and the audience loved it.'

sidecar

3 tablespoons caster (superfine) sugar
60 ml (2 fl oz/¹/₄ cup) good brandy
20–25 ml (¹/₂–³/₄ fl oz) Cointreau
2 or 3 fresh limes, juiced
sugar and lime zest, to serve

First stir 3 tablespoons of sugar and 3 tablespoons of boiling water together until dissolved, then add the brandy, Cointreau and lime juice. Add some ice and shake well. Taste a little — you may want to add some more lime to give it an edge. Serve up in a martini glass with a sugar rim and a lime zest twist.

Serves 1

'This recipe is genius and simplicity and it's totally unexpected. If you take it out to the table when you're preparing the sugar, it also creates amazing theatre. It's a really simple recipe that just needs three ingredients — a nice fresh pineapple, some mint and some sugar. Anyone can do it and it's better than a load of fancy desserts I've eaten in restaurants.'

pukka pineapple with bashed-up mint sugar

1 ripe pineapple
plain (natural) yoghurt, to serve
4 heaped tablespoons caster
(superfine) sugar
1 handful of fresh mint

Buy yourself a ripe pineapple. It should smell slightly sweet and you should be able to remove the leaves quite easily. Cut both ends off and peel the skin with a knife, removing any little black bits. Then cut the pineapple into quarters and remove the slightly less tasty core, which I usually discard or suck on while preparing the rest of the dish. Finely slice your quarters, lengthways, as thin as you can. Lay out flat in one or two layers on a large plate. Don't refrigerate this — just put it to one side.

Take the plate to the table after dinner with a pot of yoghurt that can be passed round, then return with a pestle and mortar with the sugar in it. Your family or guests will probably think you've gone mad, especially if you ignore them while you do this, but pick the mint leaves and add them to the sugar. Bash the hell out of it in the pestle and mortar at the table. You'll see the sugar change colour and it will smell fantastic. It normally takes about a minute to do if you've got a good wrist action. Sprinkle the mint sugar over the plate of pineapple — making sure you don't let anyone nick any pineapple before you sprinkle the sugar over. What a fantastic thing. If you have any leftovers, you could always make a piña colada with them.

Serves 4

index

A

A Book of Middle Eastern Food, 148
Alexander, Stephanie, 54, 149, 157, 158,
    176–9, 208
Allen, Darina, 54, 207–9
Allen, Myrtle, 207, 208
apple cake, English, 41
apricot tart, emergency, 204, **205**
artichokes, 194

B

Baghdad eggs, 181
baked mushroom bruschetta, **170**, 171
baked plaice or dover sole with herb
    butter, **213**, 214
Ballymaloe brown yeast bread, 211
Ballymaloe Cookery School, 207, 208
Barossa region, 158
bean sprouts, stir-fried with yellow beans,
    garlic and chillies, 114
beef
    braised beef with carrots, 70
    braised beef shin with a hot and sour
        salad, 222, **223**
Beer, Maggie, 149, 157–9, 176, 218
bills, Darlinghurst, 43–4, 45
Bilson, Gay, 65, 176
Blue Water Grill, Bondi Beach, 188
Boetz, Martin, 129, 217–19
braised beef with carrots, 70
braised beef shin with a hot and sour
    salad, 222, **223**
braised pork hock with dark soy sauce, 190
bread
    Ballymaloe brown yeast bread, 211
    coconut bread, 49
British food, 119, 168, 198

C

Campbell, Joan, 22–5
capsicums, sicilian, **59**, 60
caramel custard with grilled banana, 225
Carluccio, Antonio, 167–9
Carluccio, Priscilla, 167–9
Cazals, Jean, 227
cheese, little filo cheese rolls, **150**, 151
chicken
    chicken savoyarde, 56
    chinese red-cooked chicken, 81, **82**
    chook roasted with garlic and
        verjuice, 160
    free-range chicken schnitzel with
        tomato and preserved lemon salad,
        50, **51**
    grilled balsamic chicken with limes, 132
    roasted chicken with pine nut and
        raisin pilaf, 152, **153**
    salad of chicken and pomelo, 110
chickpea salad, 90
chickpeas, 90
chicory, caper and smoked salmon salad,
    122
Chinese red-cooked chicken, 81, **82**
chocolate brownies, my very good recipe,
    39, 40
chook roasted with garlic and verjuice, 160
chorizo, squid and beans, **83**, 84
Christie, Sam, 217
Clarkes, Kensington, 119
coconut bread, 49
Collingwood Kitchen Garden Project, 179
Conran, Terence, 44, 63–5, 128, 167, 168,
    197, 228
Contaldo, Gennaro, 228–9
crisp salted pork and cuttlefish salad,
    220, 221
crushed raspberry semifreddo, **134**, 135
curry
    green curry of prawns, 224
    sour orange curry of prawns with
        betel leaves, 111, **112**
    curry-leaf-crusted snapper on roast
        sweet potato with smoked coconut
        tamarind broth and plantain chips,
        141, **142**

D

dashi, 201
David, Elizabeth, 55, 64, 148, 149, 158, 179,
    227
Day-Lewis, Tamasin, 53–5
de Blank, Justin, 34, 118
desserts
    caramel custard with grilled banana, 225
    crushed raspberry semifreddo, **134**, 135
    emergency apricot tart, 204, **205**
    English apple cake, 41
    Eton mess, 71
    fig galette, **163**, 165
    green gooseberry and elderflower
        compote, 215
    konafa à la creme, 155
    lavender pear ice cream, **124**, 125
    mangosteen, lychees and rambutans
        in perfumed syrup with green
        mango and deep-fried shallots,
        113, 115
    oven-baked tamarillos with whipped
        cream and chocolate tofu and den
        miso cake, 145

desserts *continued*
    passionfruit tart, **193**, 195
    pukka pineapple with bashed-up
        mint sugar, 234, **235**
    queen of nuts cake with braised
        peaches, **183**, 185
    quince and pralinéed almond ice
        cream, 61
    simple plum tarts, 80
    summer berry jelly, **94**, 95
    summer strawberry soufflés, **30**, 31
    zabaglione with muscatel, 175
drinks
    pink gin, **100**, 101
    sidecar, 233
    striped milkshakes, 133
duck
    duck pho, 92, **93**
    duck salad, 26, **27**
    grilled duck breast, 180
    warm duck breast salad with crackling
        croutons, 91
Dupleix, Jill, 45, 72–5, 217
Durack, Terry, 45, 72–5, 217

E
eggplant and capsicum, roasted, with
        yoghurt and pine nuts, 154
eggs
    Baghdad eggs, 181
    scrambled eggs, 45, **46**, 47
emergency apricot tart, 204, **205**
English apple cake, 41
Eton mess, 71

F
Fairlie-Cuninghame, Sue, 22, 24
fantastic fish pie, **230**, 231
fig galette, **163**, 165
filo pastry, 151
fish pie, fantastic, **230**, 231
Flynn, Trevor, 98
free-range chicken schnitzel with
        tomato and preserved lemon salad,
        50, **51**
fusion cooking, 137–8

G
Good Food Guide (*Sydney Morning Herald*),
        72, 187, 217–18
Gordon, Peter, 137–9
Gould, Kevin, 96–9
Granger, Bill, 43–5, 63, 89
Gray, Rose, 228

green curry of prawns, 224
green gooseberry and elderflower
        compote, 215
grilled balsamic chicken with limes, 132
grilled duck breast, 180

H
haddock with crumbs and tarragon, 37, **38**
Hallegua, Queenie, 147
Hanger, Catherine, 25
Harriott, Ainsley, 198
Hay, Donna, 44, 45, 89, 126–9, 198
Henderson, Fergus, 65, 168
Hendy, Alastair, 197–9
Home Cook, 198
honey and chilli prawns in lettuce leaves,
        120, **121**
Hopkinson, Simon, 63
Hotel du Midi (Mme Barratero),
        Lamastre, 64

I
ice cream
    lavender pear, **124**, 125
    quince and pralinéed almond, 61
Irish colcannon soup, 210, **212**

J
jelly, summer berry, 94, 95
kecap manis, 217

K
kangaroo tail pie, 164
Kapoor, Sybil, 116–19
konafa à la creme, 155
koushary, 103
Kuni's, Melbourne, 138

L
lamb
    massaged shoulder of lamb, 104, **105**
    slashed roast lamb, **78**, 79
    walnut and fig braised lamb, 203
lavender pear ice cream, **124**, 125
Lawson, Nigella, 176
Lindsay House, Soho, 98
linguine with lemon and basil, 36
little filo cheese rolls, **150**, 151
lobster sandwich, 48
Locatelli, Giorgio, 88, 147, 168
Loftus, David, 116
Longrain, Surry Hills, 217–18, 219
Love, London, 99
Lowe, Jason, 147

M
mangosteen, lychees and rambutans in
        perfumed syrup with green mango
        and deep-fried shallots, **113**, 115
Mason, Angela, 198
massaged shoulder of lamb, 104, **105**
Mezzo, Paris, 64
miso paste, 144
mixed leaf salad with mozzarella, mint,
        peach and prosciutto, 232
mushrooms, 168
    baked mushroom bruschetta, **170**, 171
    mushrooms on toast, 202
my very good chocolate brownie recipe,
        39, 40

N
nahm, Mayfair, 107–8, 109
Neal Street Restaurant, Covent Garden,
        167, 168
noodles
    one-bowl noodles, **200**, 201
    ramen noodles with creamed sesame
        sweetcorn, crisp tofu and toasted
        walnuts, 140
stir-fried squid and prawns with squid-
        ink noodles, speck, chilli and
        coriander, 191, **192**
Norman, Jill, 138

O
Oliver, Jamie, 55, 129, 227–9
one-bowl noodles, **200**, 201
orecchiette with cauliflower and
        anchovy, 85
oven-baked tamarillos with whipped
        cream and chocolate tofu and den
        miso cake, 145
oysters rockefeller, **66**, 67

P
passionfruit tart, **193**, 195
pasta
    linguine with lemon and basil, 36
    orecchiette with cauliflower and
        anchovy, 85
    spaghettini with tomato sauce, 174
    studio pasta, 130, **131**
Patten, Marguerite, 197
pea and ham soup, 68, **69**
Perry, Neil, 72, 187–9
Perry-Smith, George, 53
Pheasant Farm Restaurant, Barossa, 158

pheasant, roasted with sage, orange and
juniper berries, 161, **162**
pink gin, **100**, 101
plum tarts, simple, 80
pork
braised pork hock with dark soy
sauce, 190
crisp salted pork and cuttlefish salad,
220, 221
pork belly hot-pot with chilli, baby
beetroot, morels and miso, **143**, 144
prawns
green curry of prawns, 224
honey and chilli prawns in lettuce
leaves, 120, **121**
prawn salad, 29
sour orange curry of prawns with
betel leaves, 111, **112**
Public, New York, 138, 139
pukka pineapple with bashed-up mint
sugar, 234, **235**

Q
quails, truffled, with balsamic sauce, 172,
173
queen of nuts cake with braised peaches,
183, 185
quince and pralinéed almond ice cream,
61

R
ramen noodles with creamed sesame
sweetcorn, crisp tofu and toasted
walnuts, 140
Ramsay, Gordon, 198
red-cooking, 81
rice
koushary, 103
roasted chicken with pine nut and
raisin pilaf, 152, **153**
Richmond Hill Café and Larder, 178
Ripe, Cherry, 86–9, 107, 128
River Café, Hammersmith, 227, 229
roasted chicken with pine nut and raisin
pilaf, 152, **153**
roasted eggplant and capsicum with
yoghurt and pine nuts, 154
roasted pheasant with sage, orange and
juniper berries, 161, **162**
Rockpool, The Rocks, 72, 187, 188, 189
Roden, Claudia, 147–9, 157
Roper, Mark, 228

S
saba, 172
salad of chicken and pomelo, 110
Schofield, Leo, 24
scrambled eggs, 45, **46**, 47
seafood
baked plaice or dover sole with herb
butter, **213**, 214
chicory, caper and smoked
salmon salad, 122
chorizo, squid and beans, **83**, 84
curry-leaf-crusted snapper on roast
sweet potato with smoked
coconut tamarind broth and
plantain chips, 141, **142**
fantastic fish pie, **230**, 231
haddock with crumbs and tarragon,
37, **38**
lobster sandwich, 48
salmon in a light, fragrant broth, 76, **77**
spanner crab *au naturel* with winter
vegetables, 194
squid with bronze skin, **182**, 184
stir-fried squid and prawns with
squid-ink noodles, speck, chilli
and coriander, 191, **192**
whitebait with an Asian flavour, 28
see also prawns
semifreddo, crushed raspberry, **134**, 135
shallots, deep-fried, 115
Sicilian capsicums, **59**, 60
sidecar, 233
simple plum tarts, 80
slashed roast lamb, **78**, 79
Slater, Nigel, 32–5, 197
Slow Food Movement, 208, 209
Smith, Drew, 119
snapper, curry-leaf-crusted snapper on
roast sweet potato with smoked
coconut tamarind broth and
plantain chips, 141, **142**
soup
Irish colcannon, 210, **212**
pea and ham, 68, **69**
sour orange curry of prawns with betel
leaves, 111, **112**
spaghettini with tomato sauce, 174
spanner crab au naturel with winter
vegetables, 194
Stephanie's, Melbourne, 176–7
Stewart, Martha, 129
stir-fried bean sprouts with yellow
beans, garlic and chillies, 114

stir-fried squid and prawns with squid-
ink noodles, speck, chilli and
coriander, 191, **192**
striped milkshakes, 133
studio pasta, 130, **131**
Sugar Club, Notting Hill, 137–8
Sukarnoputri, Megawati, 218
summer berry jelly, **94**, 95
summer strawberry soufflés, **30**, 31
Summers, Kevin, 34

T
tamarillos, 145
Thai Food, 108–9
The Book of Jewish Food, 147, 148
The Cook's Companion, 178, 179
The Hole in the Wall, Bath, 53
The Providores, London, 138
The Riverside, Helford, 53
The Soup Kitchen, London, 64
Thompson, David, 107–9, 129, 218
Tinslay, Petrina, 126, 128
tofu, ramen noodles with creamed
sesame sweetcorn, crisp tofu and
toasted walnuts, 140
tomato, goat's camembert and herb tart,
57, **58**
tomatoes with a love injection, 102
truffled quails with balsamic sauce, 172,
173
Two Fat Ladies, 198

V
veal burgers with grilled red onions and
chips, 123

W
walnut and fig braised lamb, 203
warm duck breast salad with crackling
croutons, 91
Waters, Alice, 118, 208
whitebait with an Asian flavour, 28

Y
yeast, 211

Z
zabaglione with muscatel, 175
Zafferano, London, 147

Published by Murdoch Books Pty Limited.

AUSTRALIA
Murdoch Books
Pier 8/9, 23 Hickson Road,
Millers Point NSW 2000
Phone: +61 (0)2 8220 2000
Fax: +61 (0)2 8220 2558

Chief Executive: Juliet Rogers
Publisher: Kay Scarlett

Concept and design: Marylouise Brammer
Project manager and editor: Janine Flew
Photographer: Petrina Tinslay
Food stylist: Emma Knowles
Hair and make-up: Anthea Clarke, David Novak-Piper
Food preparation: Joanne Glynn, Mandy Sinclair
Production: Megan Alsop

Printed by C&C Offset Printing.
PRINTED IN CHINA. First printed in 2005.

UK
Murdoch Books UK Limited
Erico House, 6th Floor North,
93–99 Upper Richmond Road
Putney, London SW15 2TG
Phone: + 44 (0) 20 8785 5995
Fax: + 44 (0) 20 8785 5985

ISBN 1-74045-595-9

National Library of Australia
Cataloguing-in-Publication Data

Whitaker, Neale.
    The accidental foodie.
    Includes index.
    ISBN 1 74045 595 9.
    1. Cooks — Biography. I. Title.
    641.50922

The recipes in this book are the copyright of the individual writers. Some have been published previously, and are reprinted here with the kind permission of the following:
Stephanie Alexander: Squid with bronze skin from *Stephanie's Journal* (Viking, 1999); Grilled duck breast, Baghdad eggs and Queen of nuts cake from *The Cook's Companion* (Lantern/Penguin, 1996); Braised peaches from *Stephanie's Seasons* (Allen & Unwin, 1992). Martin Boetz: All recipes copyright © *Longrain Modern Thai Food* (Hardie Grant Books, 2003). Antonio Carluccio: Baked mushroom bruschetta from *Antonio Carluccio's Complete Mushroom Book* (Quadrille Publishing Ltd, 2003); Zabaglione with muscatels from *Invitation to Italian Cooking* (Headline, 2005); Truffled quails and Spaghettini with tomato sauce copyright © Antonio Carluccio. Terence Conran: All recipes copyright © Terence Conran/Conran Octopus. Alastair Hendy: All recipes copyright © Alastair Hendy. Jamie Oliver: Fantastic fish pie and Mixed leaf salad with mozzarella, mint, peach and prosciutto from *The Return of the Naked Chef* (Penguin, 2002), Pukka pineapple with bashed-up mint sugar and Sidecar from *Happy Days with the Naked Chef* (Penguin, 2004). Nigel Slater: All recipes copyright © Nigel Slater. David Thompson: All recipes from *Thai Food* (Penguin, 2002).

The publisher also wishes to thank John Brown Citrus Publishing for permission to use quotes from *Food Illustrated* (now *Waitrose Food Illustrated*), and Jill Norman for permission to use the quote on page 6 from *An Omelette and a Glass of Wine*, by Elizabeth David (Penguin, 1986).

IMPORTANT: Those who might be at risk from the effects of salmonella poisoning (the elderly, pregnant women, young children and those suffering from immune deficiency diseases) should consult their doctor with any concerns about eating raw eggs.